PIONEER KITCHENS

OUR HERITAGE

FROM MANY LANDS

By
Southern Alberta Pioneers

Cover Photograph: Mary Fraser, Fort Chipewyan, ca. 1903

PIONEER KITCHENS – OUR HERITAGE FROM MANY LANDS
By Southern Alberta Pioneers

First Printing — September 1995

Copyright © 1995 by
Southern Alberta Pioneers and Their Descendants
3625 - 4th Street S.W.
Calgary, Alberta
Canada T2S 1Y3

Canadian Cataloguing in Publication Data

Main entry under title:

Pioneer kitchens

Includes index.
ISBN 1-895292-68-9

1. Cookery, Canadian.   2. Cookery.   3. Frontier and
pioneer life – Canada.   I. Mair, Edweena, 1906-
II. Southern Alberta Pioneers and Their
Descendants (Organization)

TX715.6.P56 1995   641.5971   C95-920200-5

Photographs courtesy of Glenbow Museum, Calgary, Alberta

Illustrations, cover and heading page design by:
Helen Mackie,
Calgary, Alberta

Designed, Printed and Produced in Canada by:
Centax Books, a Division of PrintWest Communications Ltd.
Publishing Director: Margo Embury
1150 Eighth Avenue, Regina, Saskatchewan, Canada S4R 1C9
(306) 525-2304 FAX: (306) 757-2439

TABLE OF CONTENTS

Many of these recipes are original, having been brought from the home-lands of our pioneers. Others have been modified by their descendants for use in the kitchens of today.

HISTORY OF THE SOUTHERN ALBERTA PIONEERS AND THEIR DESCENDANTS

In the early 1900s, a group of men and women, having been in Southern Alberta prior to 1890, celebrated each year when the work was done by holding a special ball. The first was in 1907.

During the 1920s, the Rotary Club suggested to this group that they organize and become certified as a nonprofit association. This advice was followed and, in January of 1922, The Southern Alberta Pioneers and Old-Timers' Association was formed.

Included in membership were all those whose predecessors had arrived in that part of Canada known as the Province of Alberta, lying south of Township 40 as far as the United States border, prior to December 31st, 1890.

In the beginning there were two separate organizations, one for men and the other for women. In 1964 they joined to form one association.

The husband or wife of a pioneer was later accepted as an associate member. Minimum age to join was 21 years.

In 1954 property was leased from the City of Calgary and a log building erected at 3625 Fourth Street Southwest, in memory of the original pioneers. This Memorial Building is the centre of activities.

In March 1974 the name of the organization was officially changed to The Southern Alberta Pioneers and Their Descendants. The age for membership was lowered to 18 years.

The objects of the association are:
(1) To collect and preserve information in connection with the early settlement and subsequent history of the association.
(2) To collect and preserve, in authentic form, a library of books, pamphlets, maps, charts, manuscripts, papers, paintings, photographs and other materials illustrative of the history of the Province of Alberta.
(3) To rescue from oblivion the memory of its early pioneers and to preserve narratives of their exploits, perils and adventures.
(4) To, in all appropriate matters, advance the interest and perpetuate the memory of those whose sagacity, energy and enterprise induced them to settle in the West.

Dedication

Our Pioneers came from many lands in search of a better life. They travelled across the vast prairies and settled in the shadows of the Rocky Mountains. Settling in the area, they met the challenges of a new country and remained to enjoy the sense of freedom and a new way of life. We dedicate this book to them.

FIRST PEOPLE

Naomi Little Walker, Blackfoot, late 1890s

First People

The First People lived off the land. They were known to have the highest consumption of meat of any race. Their diet consisted of wild meat and fowl. Animal hides were stretched with the underside exposed to obtain as much meat as possible. The meat was either dried, boiled, or cooked over an open fire. Fowl was put on a stick over the fire and turned often until tender. Rabbits were often boiled.

Wild onions, growing near the Rocky Mountains, and wild parsnips were boiled, with the vegetable water and meat broth used for soups.

Little salt and pepper was used. Bear lard was the most common fat. They had no fermentation.

Wild berries were eaten for dessert. Mint tea, from leaves gathered in the Rocky Mountains, was their main beverage.

At feasts, it was traditional to sit on the floor around the food, leaving enough space to walk. Each person had a little container into which they put a little of the food from their plate, to be saved for Manitou (Indian spirits or God).

Recipes for berry soups and pemmican date back hundreds of years. Created to make use of limited supplies and ingredients available to the Indians of Alberta, the recipes are a lesson in simplicity. Indian fried bread was concocted about the 1830s, when cast-iron pans became available. Prior to the pans, bits of dough were wrapped around a stick and cooked over the fire.

Generally speaking, the Plains Indians were nomadic. They moved from place to place following their food to areas of plenty. They ate mostly buffalo and some other wild meat such as deer, elk, antelope and bighorn sheep, which were the best choice in spring, as they are one of the few animals to retain much body fat after a meagre winter diet.

Wasting virtually nothing of the animal, they fashioned bones into tools or scraping instruments for cleaning hides. Antlers and horns became tools and ladles or cups. The rest of the animal was eaten and supplemented with roots such as turnip and wild carrot, hearts of Canadian thistle, and wild berries such as bow berries, gooseberries, strawberries and cactus berries. One berry variety or another was available fresh from spring to fall. Rose hip tea contributed high levels of vitamin C.

Rose Hip Tea

Collect wild rose hips when they are bright red, soon after the first frost in late summer or early fall. Dry thoroughly and carefully remove seeds from hips, discarding seeds. Crumble the outer shells of the hips and boil with water. Add honey to taste.

Bannock

Bannock didn't appear in the Plains Indian diet until the fur trade began to flourish in the middle 1800s. Originally a Scottish recipe, it was quickly adopted by the natives, along with the use of sugar, salt, tea and other imported goods such as cloth and copper pots.

Open a bag of flour, scoop out a hole twice the size of your fist. Into hole pour 1 cup of water and start stirring with your finger. Water will absorb flour and become pasty. Add a sprinkling of baking powder. Continue mixing until you can lift out a round lump of dough. Grease a frying pan and pat dough into it and fry slowly.

How To Cook Bannock with Currants   *(Cree)*

6	cups flour	
1½	cups lard	
3	tbsp. baking powder	

1	tbsp. salt
2	cups currants
3-4	cups water

Mix flour with lard by your hand. Add baking powder, salt and currants. Add water and make a dough. Place dough in 2, 8" square cake pans. Bake in oven for 30-40 minutes. Makes 8-10 servings. Serve with butter and berry jam.

Note: Can be baked in 2 round pans, then cut in wedges.

Fry Bread

2	cups flour
1	tsp. baking powder
½	tsp. salt

1	tbsp. sugar
¾	cup water

Mix first 4 ingredients, add water. Dough will be thick. Roll into small balls, flatten. Fry in butter on stove or over an open fire. Turn when lightly browned. Serve hot.

Indian Rice Bread

3 eggs
2½ cups milk
2 cups white Indian meal (cornmeal)
1 cup cold cooked rice

1 oz. butter, melted
1 tsp. salt
2 heaping tsp. baking powder

Beat eggs until light, add to milk, then add meal, rice, butter and salt. Beat well. Stir in baking powder. Grease 3 round shallow pans. Divide mixture, place in hot oven and bake 30 minutes Serve hot.

Mrs. Black Eagle, Mrs. Buck Running Rabbit, Mrs. Wolf Leg, n.d.

Wild Rice Spoon Bread

1 cup wild rice, cooked
¼ cup cornmeal
2 cups buttermilk
½ tsp. baking soda

1 tsp. salt and/or seasoning
to taste
2-3 eggs, beaten
2 tbsp. butter, melted

Do not overcook rice. Combine all ingredients, one at a time in order given. Place batter in greased casserole or baking dish. Bake in 325°F oven 1 hour.

Note: Wild rice is native to North America. It is grown primarily in Northern Canada, and is a favourite in Native dishes.

Dried Meat (First People)

3 lbs. flank or roast   salt to taste

Cut meat into thin strips (not too thick or meat will spoil). Salt pieces of meat with small amount of salt. Too much salt will turn meat white and cause it to lose flavour. Hang meat on lines or racks and let dry completely, about a week, depending on dryness desired. Turn meat over every day. Dried meat can be boiled, eaten fresh, or crushed to make pemmican.

Pemmican (First People)

5   cups crushed dried meat   ¼ cup shortening
3½ cups dried chokecherries, crushed   ¼ cup sugar (optional)

Mix dried meat, add chokecherries and shortening, mix thoroughly. Stir in sugar, mix well again and serve.

Hard-Grease Pemmican (First People)

Dig a long grave-like hole in the ground. Make a fire in the hole and place willows across the top. Spread meat over willows. After meat is cooked and cooled, pound it until it is a pulp.

Cut the tallow and hard fat from the animal into small pieces and cook or render. Pour the boiling tallow on the pounded meat, about pound for pound. Stir the mass thoroughly, until all the meat is saturated with the hot grease.

Make bags from the prepared hide and sew with sinew. Now shovel the hot mass of meat and grease into the bags. Sew up quickly. Choose a level piece of ground, shape the bags and turn until hard and cooled. A bag 30" long, 18" wide and 8" thick will weigh 120 to 135 pounds.

Hard-grease Pemmican will keep for years in this state.

Venison Or Moose Chasseur   *(First People)*

4-6 lbs. venison or thick pieces of moose
  1 cup claret wine
  1 cup water
1½ tsp. salt
  6 peppercorns or 2 chilies
  1 bay leaf

 10 whole cloves
  1 tsp. allspice
  1 medium onion, sliced
  ¼ cup chopped onion
  ½ cup claret wine

Place meat in an acid-resistant container. Mix together all ingredients, except meat and second quantities of onion and wine. Pour marinade over roast, steaks or game and marinate for 2 days. Remove meat and dry well. Set aside marinade. Brown meat on all sides in fat. Add the ¼ cup chopped onion and ½ cup wine. Cover and simmer 2-3 hours. Add water as needed to keep simmering. Strain marinade and add to meat during last 15 minutes of cooking. Remove meat and thicken gravy with flour and water. Serve gravy over thick slices of roast, steak or sliced game.

Doreen Turning-Robe
- Granddaughter of Chief David Crowchild

Blood warriors and wives, 1892

Fried Whitefish   *(First People)*

2-3 lbs. whitefish fillets
  1 cup cornmeal
  1 tsp. salt
  ¼ tsp. pepper

  4 tbsp. bacon fat
  ½ tbsp. lemon juice
1½ tbsp. Worcestershire sauce

Roll fish in a mixture of cornmeal, salt and pepper. Heat fat in skillet, then brown fish for 5-6 minutes on each side, or until fish flakes easily. Mix lemon juice and Worcestershire sauce and sprinkle over fish just when serving.

Tongue and Turnip (Metis)

This recipe was originally made with buffalo tongue, wild herbs and roots by Cree mothers and grandmothers. Later, the Metis women substituted domestic animal tongue and garden vegetables.

1 beef tongue	1 medium turnip, cubed
2 qts. boiling water	1 medium onion, sliced
1 tsp. salt	2 tbsp. cornstarch
⅓ cup celery trimmings	salt and pepper to taste
1 small onion, sliced	mashed potatoes

Trim tongue and scrub thoroughly. Place in large pot; add boiling water, salt, celery and small onion. Bring quickly to boil, reduce heat and simmer 21/2 hours or until tender. Remove tongue. Pour liquid through sieve. Discard vegetables, return liquid to pot. When the tongue is cool, skin and cube it and return to liquid in pot. Add turnip and medium onion. Simmer until turnip is tender, about 1 hour. Thicken with cornstarch stirred to a paste with a little cold water. Season to taste. Serve over mashed potatoes. Serves 4.

Indian Pudding (Cree)

4 cups flour	½ tsp. allspice
½ lb. lard	½ tsp. cinnamon
4 tbsp. baking powder	3 cups molasses
½ tbsp. salt	1 cup brown sugar
¾ cup raisins	1 cup white sugar
½ cup currants	2½-3 cups water

Before mixing pudding, half fill a large pot with water and bring to a boil. Put flour in large dish, then add lard, mixing by hand. Add baking powder, salt, raisins, currants, allspice and cinnamon. Mix molasses, brown sugar, white sugar into water, then add to first mixture. Use a 50 lb. flour bag to cook pudding. Tie bag with string. Boil in the big pot of water 2½ to 3 hours.
Yield: About 10 servings.

Indian Pudding with Cornmeal

1 cup cornmeal	½ cup light molasses
1½ cups boiling water	1 tsp. cinnamon
1 qt. milk	½ cup raisins
1 tsp. salt	nutmeg
½ cup sugar	

Mix together all ingredients and place in deep buttered dish. Bake in 350°F oven 1-3 hours, stirring occasionally in first hour. Serve hot, with plain or whipped cream.

Indian Cake

¼ lb. butter	½ lb. sugar
1 lb. Indian meal (cornmeal)	¼ lb. raisins
boiling milk	¼ lb. currants
2 eggs	flour

Cut butter into meal, pour enough boiling milk over to make a stiff batter. Beat eggs until light. When batter is cool, add eggs and sugar. Wash and dry raisins and currants, flour them well and stir into batter. Bake in a greased loaf or cake pan in a very slow oven (250-300°F) about 2 hours.

Indian Remedy for Tuberculosis

Place a mustard poultice between pieces of flannel, then quilt the pieces together. Place flannel between shoulders because the lungs lie towards the back.

Corn – Also called Indian corn and maize. Native to tropical America. When the Americas were first discovered, Indians were growing and eating corn. Corn was grown as a staple crop by the Maya at least 2000 years ago. It was later brought to northern areas. Available on the cob, niblets, dried, ground, also pop corn, corn oil, syrup, sugar, cornstarch, in alcohol, some medicines, some varieties were used for animal feed.

Uses: vegetable, casseroles, soups, desserts.

Blackberry Dumplings

6 cups blackberries
¾ cup water
1 cup sugar
1½ tbsp. butter
2 cups flour

3 tbsp. sugar
1 tsp. salt
3½ tsp. baking powder
1 egg, lightly beaten
milk

In saucepan combine first 4 ingredients, heat slowly. Mix flour, sugar, salt and baking powder. To flower mixture add egg and enough milk to make a stiff dough. Bring blackberry mixture to boil. Drop batter by tablespoonfuls into blackberry mixture. Cover and cook 15-20 minutes.

To serve: Spoon dumplings and juice into bowls and serve with cream.

Woman with horse and travois near Gleichen, ca. 1880s

Indian Cure for Stomach Flu

Take 2 cups dry flour, tie in a cloth. Boil in water 4 hours. Cool. Will be a hard ball. Cut off outside until you come to dry flour. As the outside crust is too hard to break, scrape it to a fine powder, cook it with milk and give to patient.

A "sure cure" – old people called it "pap".

American Immigrants

The American Frontier had been settled by the mid-1880s so the last frontier was the North West Territories. Most Americans came individually and settled after 1891. The largest group of Americans were the Mormons. They were the first large body of successful farmers. Between 1896 and 1915 nearly 1 million immigrants were admitted to Canada from the United States. Many were experienced in prairie farming, all were familiar with the North American lifestyle, many had money, and were able to bring livestock and machinery. They established themselves quickly in their new surroundings.

Canadian Immigrants

Proportional Ethnic Composition – Western Canada – 1951:

British	43%		Dutch	4%
German	14% Mennonites & Hutterites		Polish	3%
Ukrainian	11%		Aboriginal	3%
French	7%		Other	8%
Scandinavian	7% Danes, Swedes, Norwegians, Icelandic, Finns			

Reports of drought, early frost, floods, discouraged immigration of large groups after 1883, but growth was steady. In the last years of the 19th century heavy rainfall was deceiving and immigration started again in earnest.

The new settlers were of almost every creed – Roman Catholic, Greek and Russian Orthodox, Presbyterian, Anglican, Methodist, Lutheran, Mennonite, Jewish, Sikh, Moslem and Buddhist. They came from aristocratic families, from the serfdoms of Europe and the overcrowded areas of Asia. All brought skills and traditions which would mould western Canada into a distinct multicultural nation. From every ethnic group came individuals who became leaders of social, scientific, artistic, athletic and political life.

Because of the mix of the settlers, western Canada became a different type of society from the predominantly French origin of Quebec or the overwhelmingly British origin societies of Ontario and the Maritimes.

Many of the social, political, religious and cultural characteristics which differentiated the Prairies from other Canadian regions have been in large part a result of the unique ethnic composition of the population. The expectations, values and beliefs which immigrants brought with them shaped politics on the Prairies. This combination played an important role in the range of political experimentation, radicalism and alienation which characterized Western Canada throughout the first half of the 20th century. In 1891, the population of Alberta was Indian – 9,000; Metis & White – 17,593 The major cities were: Edmonton – 700; Calgary – 3,876. From 1896 to the start of World War 1, homesteaders took up most of the Alberta farmland. Until 1930 half of the population of Alberta was foreign-born. 1900 to 1910; 1,250,000 immigrants came to Canada. 1910 to 1920; 2,050,000 came. Alberta's population increased from 73,000 in 1901 to 374,000 in 1911.

NORTH AMERICAN

Mrs. Alice Gardiner digging in garden of Wineglass ranch,
north of Brockett, early 1900s

Carolina Potato Bread

3 large potatoes
potato water + milk to make 2 cups
2 tbsp. butter
8 tbsp. sugar
2 tsp. salt

2 eggs, beaten
1 compressed yeast cake or
1 cup homemade yeast or
1 tbsp. granular yeast
5-6 cups white flour

Place potatoes in pot, half cover with water and boil until done. Drain, saving water; press potatoes through a sieve or mash. Scald milk with potato water, add butter, potatoes, sugar and salt; cool to lukewarm. Add eggs and yeast. (If using yeast cake, moisten slightly.) Stir in 2 cups flour, beat 5 minutes. Continue adding flour, beating constantly, until batter is a soft dough. Knead dough until light and elastic, soft but not sticky. Place in bowl, cover and let stand overnight. In morning, divide dough into 3 medium or 2 large loaf pans, cover, let rise until double in size. Bake in 350°F oven 45-50 minutes.

Modern method: When using quick rising yeast, add yeast with flour, let dough rise until double in bulk, press down, divide into loaves, let rise again until double, then bake.

Old Maritime Oatmeal Bread

2 cups rolled oats
2 cups boiling water
1 tbsp. butter
⅓ cup molasses

2 tsp. salt
1 tsp. sugar
½ cup warm water
1 tbsp. dry yeast
4½ cups flour (approx.)

Place oats in a large bowl; pour in boiling water; add butter, molasses and salt. Stir until blended; let stand until lukewarm. In a small bowl or cup, dissolve sugar in warm water; sprinkle yeast over; let stand 10 minutes until frothy. Place flour in large bowl; add oat and yeast mixture. Mix to make a soft dough (add more flour if needed). On a lightly floured board, knead dough about 10 minutes. Place in a greased bowl, cover; let rise in a warm place about 2 hours, until doubled in size. Punch dough down; divide in half; shape into 2 loaves and place in greased loaf pans. Cover, let rise again to double in size. Bake in 375°F oven 45-50 minutes, until loaves sound hollow when tapped.

Boston Brown Bread

½ cup rye meal or flour	½ tsp. salt
½ cup cornmeal	⅜ cup molasses
½ cup whole-wheat flour	1 cup sour milk or
1 tsp. baking soda	⅞ cup milk or water
	with ⅛ cup of vinegar

Mix dry ingredients, stir in molasses and milk and mix well. Grease 1 or 1½-quart mould or 2 smaller ones. Fill about ⅔ full (no more) and cover. Place on rack in kettle, add boiling water to halfway up mould. Cover kettle. Steam 3½ hours for large mould, 1½-2 hours for smaller moulds. Check water and add more when necessary to keep water at original level. Remove from kettle; uncover. Bake in 300°F oven 15 minutes. Remove from mould.

To cut: Try this old-fashioned method. Draw a string around the hot loaf, cross the ends, and pull together gently to cut off slices.

Variation: Add ½ cup raisins to batter.

Molasses Brown Bread

2 envelopes dry yeast (2 tbsp.)	½ cup white sugar
¼ cup sugar	2 tsp. salt
warm water	¼ cup soft butter
5 cups white flour	1 cup molasses
4 cups whole-wheat flour	2 eggs (optional)

Add yeast to ¼ cup sugar dissolved in 1 cup warm water. Set aside for at least 10 minutes, stirring occasionally. Mix dry ingredients together; mix in butter. Make a well and add molasses, eggs and yeast mixture. Add enough warm water to make a stiff dough. Knead 10 minutes, until smooth and pliable. Cover and let rise in warm place 2 hours. Knead down; cover and let rise again for 10 or 15 minutes. Divide dough into 4 parts; place in 4 medium loaf pans and let rise 1 hour. Bake in 350°F oven 1 hour.

Hush Puppies

2 cups cornmeal	2 tbsp. bacon drippings
1 cup flour	seasonings of choice
2 tbsp. minced onion	2 tbsp. baking powder
1 egg, lightly beaten	milk
	fat for deep-frying

Mix all ingredients with just enough milk to make a thick mixture. Wet hands to prevent sticking and roll mixture into balls about 1½" in diameter. Drop balls into hot fat; remove hush puppies when brown and drain.

Johnnycake

½ cup flour
1 cup cornmeal
1 tsp. baking powder
½ tsp. baking soda
2 tbsp. sugar

1 tsp. salt
1 cup buttermilk
1 egg
2 tbsp. shortening, melted

Sift together dry ingredients. Add milk, stir well. Beat in egg, then shortening and mix well. Pour into hot greased pan. Bake in hot (400°F) oven 20 minutes, or until golden. Best served warm.

Suggestion: Serve with maple syrup or serve as is with soup, stew, beans, chili.

Puffy Corn Fritters

1 tbsp. butter
2 cups fresh corn
¼ cup chopped onion
¼ cup flour
½ tsp. baking powder

½ tsp. salt
2 eggs, beaten
2 tbsp. milk
3 tbsp. lard or cooking oil

In saucepan melt butter. Add corn and onion. Cook for 8 minutes, stirring occasionally. Set aside. In mixing bowl, combine flour, baking powder and salt. Add eggs and milk. Mix well. Stir in slightly cooled vegetable mixture. In large skillet, heat lard (or oil). Drop corn mixture by heaping tablespoons, 4 or 5 at a time, into skillet. Flatten slightly with the back of a spoon. Cook about 4 minutes, turning once. Drain. Serve warm with meat or poultry. Makes 12, 3½" fritters.

Sopaipillas *(Puff Bread)*

Sopaipillas are filled with honey before eating. These will satisfy any cowboy's sweet tooth.

3 pkgs. yeast
1½ cups warm water
6 cups flour
6 tbsp. baking powder

1 tbsp. salt
1½ cups buttermilk
6 tbsp. vegetable oil
vegetable oil for frying

Dissolve yeast in warm water. Sift flour, baking powder and salt together. Mix in the buttermilk and oil. Add the yeast water and mix thoroughly. Let mixture rise for 1 hour and punch down. Roll out to ¼" thickness, then cut into triangles or squares. Let rise for another hour. Cook 3 or 4 at a time in very hot oil, 1 minute on each side, or until light brown. Drain well. Yield 12.

Maritime Fiddlehead Soup

2 large potatoes, peeled and diced
½ cup diced celery
1 medium onion, chopped
1 garlic clove (optional)
1 cup water
1 cup chicken stock
2 tsp. salt
pepper
2 cups fiddleheads
1-2 cups rich milk

Put all but fiddleheads and milk in a large pot. Bring to a boil, then cover and simmer 20 minutes. Add fiddleheads and simmer until they are just tender. Cool slightly, place in a bowl, a little at a time, and beat until smooth. Put back into pot and stir in enough milk to desired thickness. Heat just to boiling point (do not boil) and season to taste. Serve with more cooked fiddleheads.

Haricot Bean Soup

1 lb. haricot (Great Northern) beans
2 qts. water
2 oz. fat bacon or 1 tbsp. butter
   pinch baking soda
2 onions, diced
1 carrot, diced
1 small piece turnip, diced
2 cups milk
flour or cornstarch, to
   thicken
salt and pepper

Rinse beans and soak in cold water at least 24 hours. Stir; discard floating skins; drain. Put 2 quarts water in a kettle, add beans, bacon or butter and baking soda (to help soften beans). Boil until beans are fairly soft. When quite soft, add onions, carrot and turnip and boil 2 more hours. Add milk. If desired, thicken with a little flour or cornstarch. Add seasoning. Heat and serve.
Note: If desired, use ham stock instead of water and bacon.

Potato and Leek Soup

4 large leeks, diced
1 oz. butter
6 cups chicken stock
1 lb. potatoes, peeled and diced
salt and pepper
1 oz. flour
¼ cup milk
cheese, grated

Split leeks lengthwise and clean well, then dice. Chill in cold water 1 or 2 hours, until crisp. Fry leeks in butter until tender. Add stock, potatoes, salt and pepper. Bring to boil, then simmer about 1 hour. Mix flour and milk, stir into soup to make as thick as desired, then stir in or garnish with grated cheese. Serve hot.

Democrat load of Saskatoon pickers near Stavely, 1909

Cape Clam Chowder

1½	cups diced potatoes	2 cups rich milk
2	medium onions, chopped	salt and pepper
1	cup water	1½ tbsp. butter
1	cup cooked clams with liquid	

Cook vegetables in water until tender. Add clams and liquid. When hot add milk; reheat, but do not boil. Stir in seasonings. Just before serving add butter.

Maine Clam Chowder

¼	lb. salt pork, in ¼" cubes	1 qt. cold milk
2	medium onions, coarsely chopped	4 tbsp. flour
1	qt. shucked clams	salt (if needed) and pepper
8	medium potatoes, in small cubes	dash of thyme

Brown pork in kettle, add onions and cook 3 minutes. Lay clams and potatoes in alternate layers over onion. Add enough cold water to cover. Heat to boiling, then cover and simmer until potatoes are tender. Uncover, add milk and heat to boiling. Add flour, mixed to a smooth paste with cold water, and continue boiling until chowder thickens as desired, stirring steadily. Season to taste. Serves 8.

Wild Duck

duck(s)
1 small onion, halved
raw cranberries

butter
salt
water

To prepare ducks, pick, draw and singe as for chicken. Dry inside and out with a towel. Rub breast lightly with onion; put several uncooked cranberries and butter, about the size of a walnut, inside each duck before cooking. Tie down wings and legs. Place duck(s) in baking dish; add salt and water to pan. Baste each duck well with butter, put in hot oven (400°F) and bake about 45 minutes. Baste occasionally. Serve with the pan gravy poured over the birds. Wild ducks are better when not stuffed. Serve with currant jelly.

Potted Birds

6 prairie chickens or pigeons
¼ lb. bacon
2 tbsp. flour
2 cups stock or water

1 tsp. salt
pepper
bay leaf
1 onion, sliced
1 tbsp. Worcestershire sauce

Singe, draw and truss birds. Cook bacon, drawing out all fat. Dust birds thickly with flour; place breast down in hot bacon fat. Cook until browned on all sides; place in stew pot or casserole. Add 1 tbsp. flour to fat in pan; add stock and remaining ingredients. Bring to boil and pour over birds; cover. Bake in 325°F or 350°F oven at least 2 hours.

Marinated Wild Game Roast

1 cup beef broth
1 tbsp. whole spice
¾ tsp. poultry seasoning
1 cup white wine

1½ tbsp. lemon juice
1 tsp. salt
1 tsp. minced onion
roast of choice

Combine all ingredients except meat. Heat, but do not boil. Place meat in close-fitting dish. Pour in marinade and let stand for 24 hours, turning several times. Remove meat and wipe clean. Brown meat and return to marinade and cover. Bake in 325°F oven for 2-3 hours.

Stuffed Roast Venison in Red Wine

hind quarter of venison, about 10 lbs.
salt and pepper
seasonings of choice
½ cup oil
1 green pepper, chopped
1 onion, chopped
2 celery stalks, chopped

4 garlic cloves, minced
1 cup red wine
4 strips bacon
1 tbsp. flour
8 oz. mushrooms, sliced
1 tbsp. chopped green onions
 and tops
1 tbsp. chopped parsley

Cut a pocket along leg bone from large end and almost to small end. Season inside the pocket well and rub outside of roast with oil. Place in roasting pan, then fill pocket with all chopped vegetables except onion tops, parsley and mushrooms. Pour wine over roast and place bacon on top. Cover and bake in 300°F oven, 3-4 hours, until tender. Remove from pan. Take ¼ cup juices from pan, stir in flour and return to pan along with mushrooms, onion tops and parsley. Mix with pan juices. Place over high heat; cook 5 minutes, until gravy thickens. Return roast to pan, with gravy, and cook about 5 minutes to brown. Serve hot.

Binder operating on Basilici ranch, Kew, 1913

Early Canadian Drinks

"Caribou" – mixture of white wine (probably dandelion wine) and gin.

"Swish" – homemade rum from Newfoundland

"Spruce Beer" – mixture of spruce boughs, molasses and yeast.

"Hootch" – mixture of sourdough and sugar from the Yukon.

A variety of homebrews or "white lightening" made across the country, included beers, ciders, wines and whiskies or "moonshine".

Dandelion

Amongst our pioneers was a familiar plant – the dandelion. The dandelion came to North America in the 1700s, as a supplement to the high protein and fat diet of the fur traders.

On the prairies some dandelions were cultivated in small gardens, protected from predators by chicken wire. It was possible for prairie children to grow up never having seen a dandelion.

This versatile plant has been used in many ways:

1. In spring its young green leaves are used for salad.

2. The blossoms are washed well and dried, dipped in beaten egg and water, then in fine cornmeal, and sautéed in ¾ cup butter or oil until brown. The blossoms can also be used in casseroles instead of mushrooms.

3. Blossoms are washed and dried to make wine.

4. To 1 quart of well-washed blossoms add 5 cups water, bring to a boil; drain; add 1 pkg. pectin to liquid. Boil; add 4 cups of sugar and bring to a boil. Pour into jars. This jells very quickly and tastes like honey.

5. Dandelion roots, dried and ground, can be used to make coffee.

Edible Flowers

The culinary use of flowers dates back thousands of years. The first recorded use was nearly 200 years before the Christian era. In the Far and Middle East – rose and orange blossoms have always been used; in Mediterranean areas – zucchini and squash flowers, lavender, roses, nasturtiums, jasmine, orange blossoms, hibiscus are used in custards, jams, jellies, liqueurs, wines, teas. Other blossoms are used to decorate, but can also be eaten – cornflowers, geraniums, chrysanthemums, marigolds, carnations, bell-flowers, calendula, forsythia, anise, boraqe, chives, hollyhock, impatiens, viola, lilac, peony, petunia, poppy (not opium poppy), snapdragons, tulips; top cakes with gladiola; float daylilies in soup or punch (some lilies are poisonous e.g. lily-of-the-valley – check carefully!); garnish vegetables with sweet peas; use honeysuckle to flavour cakes; add pansies to salad greens.

Note: before using any blossoms in food, rinse, then remove pistils, stamens and white part at base of petals.

Apple Dressing

2 cups soft bread crumbs
4 cups chopped apples
1 small onion, chopped
¼ cup raisins

¼ cup brown sugar
1 tsp. cinnamon
¼ cup butter

In a shallow pan, toast bread crumbs in oven. In a large bowl, combine bread with apple, onion, raisins, brown sugar and cinnamon. Drizzle melted butter over. Toss until combined. Spoon into greased casserole. Bake, covered, in 350°F oven for 40 minutes. Uncover and bake 5 more minutes to brown top. Makes 8-10 servings. Serve with pork or duck.

Note: This is a side dish not a stuffing.

Squash Mirassou

6 summer squash or zucchini
1 tsp. salt
⅛ tsp. pepper
1 tbsp. butter
1 large onion, chopped

½ cup red wine
2 cups puréed tomatoes
1 cup chopped mushrooms
    mixed herbs of choice

Wash squash, cut in cubes. Place with rest of ingredients in a pot and simmer until the squash is tender, 10-15 minutes. Serve hot with white fish or beef.

Newfie Jiggs Dinner

2 lbs. corned beef or salt beef ribs
½ lb. salt pork
8 potatoes, quartered

6 carrots, quartered
1 medium turnip, in chunks
1 medium cabbage, in wedges

Soak beef and pork in cold water overnight. In morning, drain and add fresh cold water. Bring to boil, then simmer at least 2 hours. Add vegetables, cooking until just done. Jiggs dinner is cooked and served with Pease Pudding.

Pease Pudding

1 cup yellow split peas
    salt and pepper

butter

Wash and drain peas. Place in a flour-sack-type pudding or jelly bag. Tie loosely so peas can expand. Boil in same water as Jiggs Dinner, for same length of time. Remove peas from bag; mash with butter and seasonings. Serve with Jiggs Dinner.

Codfish Cakes (1900)

cold boiled codfish
mashed potatoes
1 egg, beaten, or 2-3 tbsp. milk

pepper
butter or shortening

Shred codfish very fine and add an equal amount of mashed potatoes. Moisten with egg or milk. Season with pepper and a little butter. On floured board, make small flat cakes, flouring both sides. Fry cakes in shortening until brown.
Variation: Dip cakes in beaten egg, then in fine bread crumbs. Drop into hot fat and cook like fritters.

Newfoundland Cod Au Gratin

1 lb. cod fillets
2 tbsp. butter
2 tbsp. flour
1 cup milk

8 oz. old Cheddar cheese,
    grated
salt and pepper
grated Parmesan cheese

Place cod in baking dish. Melt the butter in a saucepan, stir in flour, then stir in milk gradually. When blended, add the cheese and stir until melted. Pour cheese sauce over cod, season to taste and sprinkle a little Parmesan on top. Bake in 350°F oven 30 minutes, or until fish is tender.

Sausage-Stuffed Beef Rolls

2 lbs. beef round
1 lb. pork sausage meat
1 handful parsley, chopped
2 tbsp. butter
⅔ cup wine or sherry

salt and pepper
⅔ cup beef stock
2 carrots, minced
2 medium onions, minced

Slice meat in pieces the size of a hand, less than ½" thick. Combine sausage and parsley. Place a portion of sausage about the size of an egg on each slice of beef. Roll up and tie both ends. Brown in butter, then add wine, seasonings, stock and vegetables. Cover and simmer gently 2½ hours. Remove, cut off strings. Thicken gravy slightly. Serve hot with mashed potatoes. Serves 4.

All-In-One Beef Dinner

2½ lbs. beef steak
    salt to taste
1 head cabbage, quartered
3 turnips, quartered

3-4 carrots, halved
3-4 parsnips, halved
4 onions, quartered
6 potatoes, quartered

Cover the beef with water; add salt when boiling; skim occasionally. Cook about ½ hour. Add the cabbage and cook 15 minutes, then add the rest of the vegetables. Bring to a boil; simmer about 2 hours. Drain; place vegetables in a baking dish and keep hot while slicing meat in thin slices.

Tourtière *(Meat Pies)*

Makes 5 or 6 pies depending on size of pie shells.

2 lbs. lean ground beef	2 tsp. cinnamon
1 lb. ground veal	½ tsp. ground cloves
1 lb. ground pork	¾ tsp. savory
1 large onion, finely chopped	1 carrot, finely grated
2 tsp. salt	1 cup bread crumbs
1½ tsp. pepper	pastry for 5-6 double-crust pies
½ tsp. thyme	

Combine the first 10 ingredients, simmer until the meat looks cooked. Drain, reserving the juice. Cool, then mix in bread crumbs and carrot. Roll the pastry and line 5-6 pie plates. Fill pastry shells. Dampen edges, fit on top crusts, crimp and seal. Cut slits in top and bake in slow (300-325°F) oven for about 1 hour. Brush with reserved juice for a nice brown top.

Tourtière *(Pork Pies)*

2 lbs. ground pork	1 tsp. each salt, mace, thyme
1 cup water	½ tsp. each dry mustard,
2 onions, chopped	allspice, nutmeg, black pepper
2 garlic cloves, finely chopped	2 cups mashed potatoes
2 tsp. crumbled sage leaves	pastry for 2, 9" double-crust pies

In a large pot, combine pork, water, onion, garlic and seasonings. Bring to boil, then lower heat and simmer, uncovered, stirring frequently, until the pork is cooked (no pink) and most of liquid cooked off, about 45 minutes. Remove from heat, stir in potatoes and cool to room temperature. Prepare pastry and line pie plates. Place half of mixture in each shell, put on top crust, trim and seal edges. Make cuts in top for steam to escape. Brush crusts with milk. Bake in 425°F oven 10 minutes, then reduce to 350°F for 25-30 minutes, until golden brown and the filling is bubbling. Serve hot with your favourite relish.

Suggestion: Brown the meat and pour off fat before combining with water, and other ingredients.

Rose Hip Jam

Vitamin C before oranges? Rose hips are high in vitamin C.

2 lbs. fresh rose hips	1 cup sugar
1¼ cups water	

Remove stems, seeds, and blossom ends from rose hips. Wash quickly; put in a pot with the water; bring to a boil, then cover and simmer ½ hour, until tender. Strain, then weigh pulp, adding 1 cup sugar for 1 lb. pulp. Bring to boil and boil 10 minutes, stirring constantly. Pour into sterilized jars, cool and seal.

Fried Salt Pork

1 lb. salt pork, thinly sliced
   flour

2 cups milk
   salt and pepper

Place pork slices in cold water, let stand 1 hour. Drain and dry. Dip each slice in flour and fry in hot frying pan until crisp. Set aside but keep warm. Drain off all but 2 tbsp. fat and stir in 2 tbsp. flour. Cook well, stirring constantly, then reduce heat and stir in milk slowly. Cook until thickened; add seasoning and pour over pork slices.

Fèves Au Lard *(Pork and Beans)*

2   lbs. white beans
½   tsp. baking soda
1   tsp. dry mustard
½   cup brown sugar

3   tbsp. molasses*
½   tsp. ginger
2   lbs. salt pork (sliced)

In an earthenware pot, soak beans overnight in cold water. In the morning, drain and pour the beans into a large cooking pot with water to cover. Add baking soda and cook until the beans are tender. Remove from heat, drain, rinse well with cold water, then add fresh cold water to cover beans. Add mustard, sugar, molasses and ginger and mix well. Transfer beans to original bean pot, alternating layers of beans with layers of salt pork. Bake in 325°F oven for 3 hours or 300°F oven for 4-5 hours.

* Use table molasses for light beans, baking molasses for dark beans.

Maple Baked Beans

     cold water
1   lb. navy or pea beans
1   lb. salt pork, sliced
1   bay leaf
1   onion, whole
3   whole cloves

1   tsp. dry mustard
1½   tsp. salt
½   tsp. pepper (or more)
⅓   cup molasses
⅓   cup maple syrup

Use a large quantity of cold water to soak beans overnight. Next day drain well. Place a layer of salt pork (save some for top) on the bottom of a bean pot, then pour in the beans. Attach bay leaf to whole onion with the cloves, then place on beans. Combine remaining ingredients and pour over beans. Pour in enough boiling water to cover beans, then place remaining salt pork on top. Cover and bake in 350°F oven 4-5 hours Uncover for the last ½ hour. Check beans occasionally during cooking and add water if needed.

Chicken 'N' Honey

6 large boneless chicken breasts

Honey Mustard Sauce:

⅔ cup butter
1 cup honey
¼-½ cup prepared mustard

1 tbsp. curry powder
dash salt

Prepare chicken. Combine and heat the sauce ingredients. Pour the sauce into a shallow dish. Place the chicken, meat side down, in the sauce. Bake, uncovered, in 375°F oven about 45 minutes, basting every 15 minutes.

French Canadian Boiled Chicken Dinner

4-5 lb. stewing chicken
½ tsp. nutmeg
1 tbsp. lemon juice
  salt and pepper
½ tsp. thyme
  melted fat
2 lbs. salt pork, lean and fat
3 qts. hot water
1 tsp. salt

½ tsp. savory
2 onions, minced
½ cup celery leaves
1 small green cabbage, quartered
12 carrots, peeled, halved
12 small onions, whole
2 lbs. yellow or green beans
12 new potatoes, scrubbed

Remove excess fat from chicken; cut the fat in small pieces and melt in saucepan. Rub chicken outside with nutmeg and lemon juice. Sprinkle inside with salt, pepper and thyme. Brown chicken in a little melted fat over medium heat, then add salt pork, water, salt, savory, onion and celery. Bring to a boil, reduce heat, cover and simmer 2 hours, or until almost done. Add cabbage, whole carrots, onions, beans tied in small bundles with coarse thread, and potatoes. Bring to a boil, cover and cook ½ hour, or until all are tender. Prepare the sauce below. To serve, place the chicken and salt pork in the centre of a warm platter, surround with vegetables and top with sauce.

Butter Sauce:

½ cup butter
½ cup finely chopped parsley

½ cup finely chopped chives

To make the sauce, melt butter, add herbs and serve hot.

Rice – It grew as a wild grass in India and Australia long before its seeds were found to be edible. Cultivated in prehistoric times in India and China, it was mentioned in Chinese history in 2800 B.C. About 2500 years ago rice was brought to the Middle East; taken to Spain by the Arabs, then gradually into Europe. In 1674 rice was brought to the American colonies and grown in several southern states. Most rice is grown in India, China, Japan and the East Indies. Available in kernels, brown (natural), white (husked), and flour and starch. Uses: main dishes, casseroles, cereals, puddings, gruel for upset stomachs, sake (rice wine); grasses (or straw) of rice plant used for hats, sandals, mats, etc.

Wild Rice – Native to North America, it is largely grown in Northern Canada. Was a staple food of early North American Indians and caused numerous wars among tribes. Early explorers and settlers learned to use wild rice. Available in kernels (dark brown) and flour.

Prairie Wheat Cake

Topping:

½	cup sugar	1	tsp. almond or vanilla flavouring
½	cup butter	1½	cups wheat, washed and
¼	cup milk		coarsely ground

Make topping first, before starting batter. Combine all the topping ingredients. Bring slowly to a boil; cook until the sugar is dissolved. Set aside until cool, then pour over batter.

Batter:

⅓	lb. butter	3	tsp. baking powder
½	cup sugar		salt
3	eggs	½	cup milk
3	cups flour	1	lemon, grated rind of

Cream butter and sugar. Add eggs, 1 at a time, beating well after each egg. Combine flour, baking powder and salt, and add alternately with the milk. Mix in lemon rind. Batter will be stiff. Press into a thin layer in a greased cake pan and spread topping over. Bake in 350°F oven 30 minutes. Cool. Split in 2 layers, then put following filling between layers.

Filling:

⅓	cup butter	1½	cups, or more, icing sugar
1	tbsp. almond flavoring		to spreading consistency
2	egg yolks		Saskatoons

Combine ingredients, except the Saskatoons, and beat well. When ready to spread between 2 cake layers, stir in Saskatoons. Icing the top of the cake is optional.

Switchel

1	*gallon water*	2	*cups brown sugar*
1½	*cups vinegar*	1	*tsp. ginger*
1	*cup molasses*		

Mix all ingredients. Pour in jug and hang in well to cool.

This cool refreshing drink was a welcome pause from haying.

Carrot Cake with Apricot Jam

2 cups sugar
1½ cups oil
4 eggs, slightly beaten
2 cups flour
2 tsp. baking soda
1 tsp. salt

2 tsp. cinnamon
3 cups grated carrots
1 cup chopped pecans
chopped almonds (optional)
apricot jam

Beat together sugar and oil, then beat in eggs. Sift dry ingredients and mix into sugar mixture. Fold in carrots and pecans. Grease tube pan and sprinkle lightly with almonds. Spoon cake mixture into pan; bake in 350°F oven for 1 hour. Cool 15-20 minutes, then turn pan upside down to turn out cake onto a serving plate. Ice cake with apricot jam.

Potato/Chocolate Cake

6 tbsp. cocoa
2 tbsp. butter
⅔ cup butter
2 cups brown sugar
4 egg yolks
2½ cups flour
2 tsp. baking powder
1 tsp. cinnamon

1 tsp. cloves
1 tsp. nutmeg
1 cup hot mashed potatoes
½ cup milk
1 cup raisins, lightly floured
1 cup nuts (optional)
4 stiffly beaten egg whites

Melt together cocoa and 2 tbsp. butter until smooth. Cream ⅔ cup butter and sugar, add cocoa mixture and beat well. Add egg yolks. Mix thoroughly. Sift together flour, baking powder and spices. Stir potatoes into cocoa mixture, alternately add flour mixture and milk, then raisins and nuts, if using. Fold in the egg whites. Spread in a greased 9 x 13" pan, bake in 350°F oven until it tests done.

Picnic, Dog Pound Creek area, early 1900s

Scripture Cake (1845)

Judges V, 25
Jeremiah VI, 20
Isaiah X, 14
I Samuel XXX, 12
Genesis, XLIII, 11
Kings X, 10

Exodus XVI, 31
Genesis XXIV, 17
I Kings IV, 22
Leviticus II, 13
Amos IV, 5

Follow Solomon's prescription for making a good boy, Proverbs XXIII, 14) and you will have a good cake (Proverbs III, 12). This type of recipe came into fashion long before Calgary was incorporated in 1875 and remained in use at serving bees and quilting parties. The recipes were given by the originator as a guessing game. The exercise genteelly tested the guests' knowledge of the Bible, their ability as cooks and further, it prevented the virtuous gathering from indulging in idle gossip!

Here is how the recipe appears when translated into modern terms:

1	cup butter	¼	tsp. each cloves, cinnamon
3	cups brown sugar		nutmeg, mace and allspice
6	eggs	2	cups raisins
¼	cup honey	2	cups chopped figs
3½	cups whole-wheat flour	1	cup slivered almonds
⅛	tsp. salt	¾	cup water
4	tsp. baking powder		

Cream butter, Add sugar and blend well. Add eggs one at a time and beat well after each addition. Beat in honey. Combine whole wheat-flour, salt, baking powder and spices in a bowl. In a separate bowl, mix raisins, figs and nuts, adding some of the flour mixture to coat fruit with flour. Stir flour into egg mixture. Alternately add fruit mixture and water, using a wooden spoon; beat well after each addition. Spoon into greased and floured tube pan. Bake in 275°F oven at least 2 hours.

Suggestion: Place a pan of water in the bottom of the oven to prevent cake drying out.

Note: Ageing only improves the rich flavour and moist texture.

Jelly Frosting

In earlier days jams and jellies were put to good use since each homemaker did her own preserving. This frosting was common at one time. Maybe it should stage a comeback!

Empty a glass of jelly into a mixing bowl and cut. Add one unbeaten egg white and mix. Then beat with a dover egg beater until stiff enough to spread on cake.

Cream Cake

1 cup heavy cream
1 cup sugar
2 eggs
1 tsp. vanilla

2 cups flour
2 tsp. baking powder
½ tsp. salt

Beat cream until fluffy. Gradually beat in the sugar. After about half has been added, add the eggs and vanilla and continue to add the sugar. Beat until mixture is very light and fluffy. Sift the flour with the baking powder and salt; fold into the cream mixture. Immediately turn into a greased and floured pan. You may use a 9 x 13" pan or 2, 8" pans. Bake at 350°F for 25 minutes for layers and 35 minutes for sheet cake.

Variation: Sour Cream Cake – this recipe does not work with commercial sour cream. To 1 cup of sweet cream add 1 tbsp. vinegar and stir well. Let stand 15 minutes. Use ½ tsp. baking soda and 1 tsp. baking powder as leavening.

Grandma's Orange Date Cake

2 cups flour
1 tsp. baking powder
  pinch salt
1 cup white sugar
½ cup butter
1 egg, beaten

1 tsp. baking soda, dissolved in
1 cup sour milk
1 cup finely cut dates
½ cup chopped walnuts (optional)
1 orange, juice and grated rind

Sift flour twice before measuring, sift again with baking powder and salt. Cream sugar and butter, blend in egg. Stir in flour mixture and milk. Stir in dates, nuts and grated orange rind (use the juice in the icing). Bake in a greased cake pan in a moderate oven until done.

Orange Icing:
½ cup white sugar   1 orange, juice of (from cake)

Blend together and pour over hot cake when it is removed from oven.

Maple Brandy Snaps

¼ cup maple syrup
¼ cup molasses
½ cup butter
1 cup flour, sifted

⅔ cup sugar
1 tsp. ground ginger
2 tsp. brandy

Combine syrup and molasses and bring to a boil. Remove from heat, add butter to melt. Sift dry ingredients; combine gradually with syrup mixture. Add brandy and stir. Drop by teaspoonfuls onto greased baking sheet. Bake in 300°F oven about 10 minutes, until flat and lacy. Loosen each cookie gently and roll it around the handle of a wooden spoon. Slide off and cool on a rack. Serve filled with whipped cream.

Suet Pastry

1 tsp. baking powder
2 cups flour
½ tsp. salt

1 cup chopped suet
1 cup cold water

All ingredients must be very cold. Sift dry ingredients, add suet and water and mix into a smooth, firm dough. Chill. Roll to make 1, 2-crust pie, or 2, 9" shells. Excellent for boiled fruit pudding, dumplings or baked or boiled meat pies.

Harvest-Time Raisin Pie *(Funeral Pie)*

2 cups raisins, washed
2 cups water
¾ cup sugar
2 tbsp. flour

½ tsp. cinnamon
1 tbsp. vinegar
pastry for 2-crust pie

Combine the raisins and water; bring to a boil; reduce heat and simmer 15 minutes. Blend sugar, flour and cinnamon, then add to raisin mixture. Stirring constantly, bring all to a boil for 1 minute, until thickened, then add vinegar. Stir, then cool slightly. Pour mixture into pie shell, cover with top crust and make 2 or 3 slits in top. Bake in 400°F oven 30 minutes, or until golden. *(This pie was served at funerals in the early days.)*

Sunflower Pie

3 eggs, beaten
½ cup brown sugar
⅔ cup dark corn syrup
2 tbsp. butter, melted

1 tsp. vanilla
1 cup roasted, salted
  sunflower kernels
1 unbaked pie shell

In a large bowl, beat together eggs, brown sugar, corn syrup, butter and vanilla. Spread sunflower kernels in bottom of pie shell. Pour on sugar mixture. Bake in 350°F oven 50-60 minutes. Cool.

Sweet Potato Pie

3 sweet potatoes
  rich pastry
1 cup brown sugar
1 cup butter, divided

¼ tsp. nutmeg
½ tsp. cinnamon
½ tsp. allspice
¼ cup spiced vinegar or
  ¼ cup vinegar

Peel and slice potatoes. Boil until about half done and save the potato water. Line baking pan with rich pie crust. Place a layer of potatoes sprinkled with sugar, butter and spices. Place on this a thin layer of pastry, repeat layers until all potatoes are used, with potato layer on top. Pour in boiling potato water until potatoes are nearly covered; add spiced vinegar and lots of seasoning. Cover with pastry and cut small slits to let out steam. Cook in 325°F-350°F oven 30-40 minutes, until crust is done and browned. Before removing from oven, brush top with butter and sprinkle with sugar. *Note:* If desired, a sliced apple or soaked dried apple slices, could be added with the potatoes.

Maple Sugar Pie

2 eggs
1 cup brown sugar
2 tbsp. flour
3 tbsp. soft butter

1 cup maple syrup
¾ cup chopped nuts (optional)
1 tsp. vanilla
1 unbaked pie shell

Beat eggs in mixing bowl until frothy, add sugar, flour and butter. Beat until smooth. Mix in syrup, nuts and vanilla. Pour into pie shell. Bake at 350°F for about 40 minutes.

Maritime Nutmeg Sauce

1 cup sugar
1 tbsp. flour
  salt

2 cups boiling water
1 tbsp. butter
1 tsp. grated nutmeg

In saucepan, mix sugar, flour and pinch of salt. Gradually add boiling water, stirring constantly. Add butter and cook 5 minutes. Remove from heat and stir in nutmeg. Serve hot on apple dumplings, berry puddings made with biscuit dough, or try on other puddings.

Apple Grunt

6 apples, peeled and sliced
⅓ cup sugar

½ tsp. cinnamon
¼ tsp. cloves

Place apples, sugar, cinnamon and cloves in a saucepan. Simmer slowly, adding a little water if necessary, until apples are just tender. Place apple mixture in a baking dish.

Biscuit Topping:
1½ cups flour
2 tbsp. sugar
3 tsp. baking powder

6 tbsp. shortening
⅔ cup milk
1 eggs, lightly beaten

Combine flour, sugar and baking powder in a mixing bowl. Cut in shortening until like cornmeal. Add milk and egg. Mix lightly. Drop by spoonfuls on top of apple mixture. Spread to cover. Bake in a 425°F oven for 20 minutes. Serve with hard sauce or cream.

Maple Sugar – Sugaring with maple is older than our country's written history and is unique to North America. Indians taught the first French settlers how to make a cut in the maple tree to draw out the sap, and to boil the liquid down to sugar. For many years this was the only kind of sweetening available to the pioneers. Because of this, most maple recipes are old. Many dishes reflect the culinary art of seventeenth-century France, when early settlers adapted their Norman dishes to Canadian ingredients. Now many of the original maple forests have disappeared, and maple products are a delicacy.

BRITISH ISLES

Shirley Rourke cooking supper in Bragg Creek

British Isles

Ireland, by the 1840s, was the most densely populated country in Europe – 8.25 million people on 13.5 million acres. In 1846-47, the Potato Famine, followed by typhus, caused huge numbers to perish. For those that lived, emigration offered the only hope for the future.

2,500 Irish families were registered as being residents of New France in 1700.

The Irish constituted the largest group in the "British Category" when the first census was taken after confederation in 1871. The Irish numbered 846,414, English – 706,369, Scots – 549,946.

An Irish-American, Nicholas Sheran, started the first coal mining at Coalbanks (now Lethbridge) in 1874.

Welsh – The first known Welshman to come to Canada was Sir Thomas Button, a naval officer who commanded an expedition in search of the Northwest Passage in 1612. In the late 19th century, the Welsh came to North America to escape large-scale unemployment resulting from economic depression in Wales.

Scots – Scottish emigration to North America started in 1760, after New France came under British rule. One of the early illustrious Scots in Western Canada was Sir Alexander Mackenzie who followed an unexplored river he called "River of Disappointment" which is now the Mackenzie River. Another, Simon Fraser, in 1808 accomplished one of the most dangerous feats in the history of Western exploration when he followed the river that bears his name to the Pacific.

English – The English have been in Canada since they sponsored John Cabot's voyage in 1497. The first English colony to be established in what is now Canada was founded in Newfoundland in 1611, by a group of fisherman from Devon, England. Some of the early English explorers in Western Canada were Martin Frobisher, Henry Hudson and William Baffin. The English formed the Hudson's Bay Company in 1760 when they learned of the potential wealth in furs in Canada. This gave them a monopoly on trade.

Until the American revolution, and the influx of United Empire Loyalists from the United States, the population of Canada was predominately French.

The opening of the Canadian Prairies attracted 188,000 English immigrants between 1901 and 1913.

English Muffins

2 cups milk	½ tsp. salt
4 tbsp. butter or lard	3 cups flour
1 yeast cake moistened in	
½ cup water	

Scald milk; add butter; cool to lukewarm and add moistened yeast, salt and 2 cups of the flour. Beat thoroughly, then slowly add remaining 1 cup of flour, beating constantly. Cover and let stand in warm place 2 hours. Heat griddle slowly; place greased muffin rings* on top. Put 2 tbsp. batter into each ring. Slowly bake 1 side, then turn them, rings included, and bake other side. When nearly done, remove rings and bake muffins slowly on griddle for 10 minutes. Serve hot or pull apart and toast.

* Clean, greased 6-8 oz. fish cans with both ends cut out will work.

Steamed Brown Bread (British)

1 coffeecupful graham flour	1 tsp. baking soda
1 coffeecupful cornmeal	½ teacupful sugar
1 coffeecupful white flour	¾ cup molasses
1 tsp. salt	2 cups sour milk

Sift together the first 3 ingredients. Sift salt, soda, sugar into flour mixture. Stir in molasses and milk. Put all in a lard pail, cover tightly, and set in a pot of boiling water. Boil steadily 2½ hours.

No-Yeast Buns

1 tsp. cream of tartar	1¼ cups flour (approx.)
1 cup sweet milk	½ tsp. baking soda dissolved in a
¼ cup sugar	little hot water
3 eggs, beaten	dash salt

Stir cream of tartar into milk and add, with sugar, to beaten eggs. Mix well, then add enough flour to make a thin batter. Add water with dissolved soda, and salt. Stir briskly, pour into buttered muffin tins with round bottoms, bake in a quick (400°F) oven. Serve hot.

Light Soda Bread (Irish)

4 cups flour	1 tsp. salt
3 tbsp. sugar	⅓ cup butter
¾ tsp. baking soda	2 eggs, beaten
1 tbsp. baking powder	1½ cups buttermilk

In a large bowl, mix dry ingredients. Cut in butter until mixture resembles coarse crumbs. Beat eggs; set aside 1 tbsp. Stir buttermilk into the rest of the eggs, then stir this wet mixture into dry mixture, blending just until flour is moistened. Place dough on lightly floured board; knead lightly, just enough to blend thoroughly. Shape into ball, place in well-greased 2-quart round casserole. In centre of ball cut a 4" diameter cross, ¼" deep. Brush dough with reserved egg. Bake in 350°F oven about 1 hour, then turn heat down to 300°F and bake another ½ hour. Cool in pan 10 minutes, then remove and cool on rack.

Variation: Add 1 cup raisins and 1 tbsp. caraway seed to dry mixture before adding egg/buttermilk mixture. This is great toasted!

Dark Soda Bread (Irish)

3 cups flour	1 tsp. salt
2 cups whole-wheat flour	2 tbsp. brown sugar
2 tsp. baking soda	2½ cups buttermilk
1 tbsp. baking powder	

In a bowl, mix all dry ingredients well, being careful to break up any lumps of brown sugar. Pour in all the buttermilk at once and stir until a soft ball is formed. Place dough on floured board and knead for a couple of minutes. Shape into 2 round loaves; place on baking sheet and press top down a bit to flatten. Sprinkle a bit of flour on top of each loaf, and with a sharp knife make a cross in slashes on top. Let stand for 10 minutes, then bake in 375°F oven 45 minutes, or until brown and crunchy.

Variation: Add ½ cup wheat germ.

Potato Bread (Irish)

4-5 lbs. old potatoes salt	3-4 cups flour

Boil potatoes with salt, then mash while warm. To make the dough, add flour and work with hands, adding enough flour to make soft dough. Form into 4 balls. Roll on floured board to ⅜" thick and cut in 8 triangles. Cook in warm-to-hot frying pan until browned on both sides.

To serve: Usually as a breakfast dish – fry in oil or bacon fat a few minutes and serve with bacon and eggs.

Albert Armstrong family outside log homestead, Conjuring Creek, 1906

Freckle Bread (Irish)

2 pkgs. dry yeast
1 cup warm potato water
½ cup warm mashed potatoes
½ cup sugar
5¼ cups flour

1 tsp. salt
2 eggs, beaten
½ cup butter, melted
1-1½ cups raisins

Dissolve yeast in potato water, then beat in potatoes, 2 tbsp. of the sugar and 1 cup of the flour. Cover and let rise 30 minutes, or until bubbly. Stir dough down and mix in remaining sugar, then salt and 1 cup of flour. Stir in eggs, butter and raisins and enough flour to make a soft dough. On lightly floured board, knead dough until smooth and elastic. Put in greased bowl, turning dough until all the surface is greased. Cover, set aside, and let rise until double in size. Cut in 4 pieces, shape into loaves. Grease 2, 5 x 9 loaf pans; place 2 loaves, side by side, across in each pan. Let rise until doubled in size. Bake in 350°F oven 35-50 minutes, or until bread tests done. Yield: 2 loaves

Scottish Oat Cakes (Scottish)

1 cup oatmeal (Scottish-type, medium)
¼ tsp. salt
¼ tsp. baking soda

1 tbsp. butter
¼ cup hot water
(no flour, except for rolling)

Mix together the dry ingredients, then rub in butter. Add hot water; use a little more, if needed. Mix. Roll thin on floured board, cut in triangles. Bake in 325°F oven about 30 minutes. Do not let them brown as they become bitter. Serve with butter and cheese. These are also good with a cheese ball.

Scottish Currant Buns   *(Scottish)*

Crust:

3 cups flour	½ cup butter or shortening
½ tsp. baking powder	½ cup cold water (approx.)

Fruit Filling:

2 cups flour	1 lb. currants
2 cups sugar	1 lb. raisins
1 tsp. ginger	¼ lb. peel
1 tsp. cinnamon	¼ lb. almonds, blanched and
½ tsp. pepper	chopped
½ tsp. cream of tartar	enough milk to moisten

Combine flour and baking powder; cut in the butter. Add just enough water to make a pliable dough. Roll into thin sheet; line a pan (the middle-sized square fruit cake pan is best) with ½ the crust. Sift dry filling ingredients together, then remaining ingredients. Spread over pastry. Lay remaining pastry on top and prick with fork. Bake at 300°F for 2½ hours.

Cardiff Cakes   *(Welsh)*

2½ cups flour	6 tbsp. unsalted butter, chilled and
⅔ cup sugar	cut in pieces
¾ tsp. ground mace	6 tbsp. vegetable shortening, chilled
½ tsp. baking powder	⅓ cup dried currants
¼ tsp. salt	5 tbsp. milk (approx.)
	1 egg

Mix first 5 ingredients in a large bowl. Add butter and shortening; rub with fingertips until mixture resembles fine meal. Add currants. Whisk 4 tbsp. milk and egg in small bowl. Add to "meal" mixture; stir until moist clumps form, adding more milk if mixture is too dry. Roll dough to ½" thick round on lightly floured board. With cookie cutter, cut 2½"-3" rounds. Use up all the dough. Heat heavy, large, well-seasoned griddle over medium-high heat. Place several rounds on griddle. Reduce heat to low; cook until cakes set and brown, turning occasionally, about 12 minutes. Serve warm or at room temperature. Makes about 17.

Crempog *(Pancakes)*   *(Welsh)*

This recipe dates back to the 18th century.

¼ cup flour	1 cup milk
¼ cup white sugar	3-4 eggs, lightly beaten
1 tsp. baking soda	large pat butter, melted
2 tbsp. cream of tartar	honey
4 tbsp. sour milk	

Place dry ingredients, in a large bowl. Add the milks, eggs and butter, blending thoroughly. Drop spoonfuls onto hot, greased pan, browning both sides. Serve hot with butter and honey.

Oxtail Soup   *(English)*

1½-2   ox joints
      seasoned flour
      beef drippings
2   medium onions, coarsely chopped

2   carrots, coarsely chopped
2   celery stalks, chopped
6   leeks, chopped
2   qts. water

Wash and dry ox joints, cover with seasoned flour and brown in hot drippings. In soup pot place joints, vegetables and water. Cover and simmer 3 hours. Meat should come off bones easily. Remove bones, skim off fat, add seasonings of choice, reheat and serve hot.

Lots O' Potato Soup   *(Irish)*

½   cup butter, melted
¾   cup flour
1½   tbsp. pepper

11   cups milk
6   medium potatoes, cooked, mashed
2   lbs. cheese, grated

In saucepan over medium heat, melt butter, add flour and pepper, then stir in 3 cups milk, stirring constantly until thickened. Stir in remaining milk and bring to boil. Cook 5 more minutes; remove from heat and stir in potatoes and cheese. Yield: 32 servings

Potato Soup   *(Scottish)*

1   lb. pork or mutton
1   ham bone
4   qts. cold water
1   onion, finely chopped

2   carrots, grated
1   celery stalk, finely chopped
4   potatoes, sliced, parboiled
      salt and pepper to taste

Cover pork and ham bone with water. Simmer; skim occasionally. When no more froth forms, add remaining ingredients. Simmer gently for 3 hours.

Cover boiled potatoes with a towel to absorb steam before mashing. Be sure potatoes are mashed thoroughly. A lump in the mashed potatoes has been compared to a button in the contribution plate. Not negotiable!!

Cock-A-Leekie Soup   *(Scottish)*

1 small fowl
2 qts. water
2 tbsp. rice, washed
1 chunk turnip
4-6 leeks, chopped

1 carrot, whole
salt
seasonings in cheesecloth bag
  (e.g. parsley, 2 cloves,
  6 peppercorns)

Simmer fowl in water until hot. Add rice, vegetables and seasonings and simmer 1 hour. Remove vegetables and bag of seasonings. If desired, remove bones, dice some of meat from fowl and stir into soup. Serve hot.

Note: If fowl is old, boil 1 hour or more before adding vegetables.

Hauling Water, Lucky Strike district, early 30s

Colcannon

Although the Irish claim Colcannon as a national dish, we get a Scots version, as well as a Devonshire one. It is one of those "homely" dishes dear to the heart of country people throughout the British Isles.

In the Irish recipe, boiled potatoes and parsnips are mashed, moistened with milk, mixed with chopped cabbage and simmered a few minutes with a little butter, salt and pepper.

In Scottish Colcannon, mash boiled carrots, turnips and potatoes. Cook and mix with chopped boiled cabbage, butter, a little brown sauce, salt and pepper.

In the Devonshire recipe, shredded boiled onion, potatoes and cabbage are mixed and browned in butter in a frying pan.

Cullen Skink (*Scottish*)

¾ lb. smoked haddock (if not available,
    Alaska smoked cod will do)
1 large onion, sliced
2 cups milk

1 lb. potatoes, cooked, mashed
salt and pepper
½ oz. butter
chopped parsley

Put fish in shallow pan and cover with water; bring to a boil. Add onion and simmer about 5 minutes, or until fish is cooked. Lift out fish and remove skin and bones; return skin and bones to water, simmer about 1 hour to make stock. Meanwhile, flake cooked fish. When stock is ready, strain, add milk and bring to a boil. Stir in fish and simmer 5 minutes. Stir in potatoes to make a creamy soup. Season with pepper and salt. Add butter and serve hot.

Oatmeal Soup (*Scottish*)

½ cup oatmeal
3 cups boiling water
1 onion, chopped
4 tbsp. butter, melted
   flour

1½ cups beef broth
1½ cups tomatoes
salt and pepper
2 tsp. sugar

In double boiler, place oatmeal and water and cook 30 minutes. Brown onion in butter. Add enough flour to thicken, stirring until smooth. Add oatmeal, broth and tomatoes. Mix thoroughly. Season to taste. Simmer until blended. Serve hot.

Parsnip Soup (*Scottish*)

6 medium parsnips
½ onion, finely chopped
1 garlic clove, finely chopped
1 tbsp. butter
2 cups chicken stock

1 tsp. lemon juice
⅛ tsp. nutmeg
⅛ tsp. curry powder
¼ tsp. marjoram
salt and pepper to taste

Peel parsnips and cook in water just to cover. When cooked, press through a sieve, including liquid. In saucepan, sauté onion and garlic in butter until golden. Add parsnip mixture, chicken stock, lemon juice and spices. Simmer on low heat to blend flavours, 15-20 minutes, and serve hot.

Hearty Scotch Broth (Scottish)

1	cup dried green peas	2	onions, chopped
½	cup barley or oatmeal	3	large carrots, diced
2-3	lbs. mutton neck or shoulder	1	cup diced turnip
2	qts. cold water	½	cup diced celery
	salt and pepper	1	tbsp. chopped parsley

Soak peas overnight. Soak barley 2 hours. Wipe meat and trim off fat. Put water in kettle, add meat, salt and pepper. Bring to a boil and skim off fat. Drain peas and barley, add with the onion to the broth. Simmer slowly for 2 hours. Cool. Skim off fat, remove bones. Cut meat off bones, dice meat and return to pot. Place back on low heat, add carrots, turnip and celery, and simmer 30 minutes, or until vegetables tender. Add more seasoning to taste. Twenty minutes before serving, skim any fat from surface and stir in parsley. Serve hot.

Scotch Broth

I couldna rest in bed this nicht
Until I wrote to put ye richt
I know a Scot ye canna be
Or else forsooth ye'd surely see
The Scotch borth recipe ye gave
Wad turn poor Rabbie in his grave.
Masel', I think it's oxtail soup
But Scotch broth it could never be
I often made it o'er the sea.
When made richt it is quite the thing
On it ye'd dance the Highland Fling,
I hope ma letter doesn't offend ye,
But the recipe I'd gladly send ye!

Rabbit Soup

	leftover rabbit and bones	¼	tsp. thyme
1	soup bone	1	bay leaf
¼	lb. salt pork	4	cups chicken broth
3	carrots, sliced	1	cup diced potatoes
1	onion, quartered	½	cup diced celery
2	garlic cloves, sliced	½	cup diced carrots
¼	tsp. parsley		

Remove rabbit meat from bones and set aside. In large pot combine all bones and salt pork. Add 3 carrots, onion, garlic, parsley, thyme, bay leaf. Cover with water, simmer until water is almost gone. Add chicken broth and simmer another 15 minutes. Strain, saving liquid. Return liquid to pot; add diced vegetables, rabbit meat and salt and pepper to taste. Heat and serve.

Bread and Butter Sauce   *(English)*

1   cup bread crumbs
2   cups milk
2   tbsp. chopped onion
6   cloves

½   tsp. salt
    pinch cayenne
2   tbsp. butter

Put breadcrumbs and milk in double boiler. In small cheesecloth bag place onion and cloves and cook with milk and crumb mixture for 30 minutes. Remove cheesecloth bag, add seasonings and butter. Serve sauce hot, with poultry or fish.

Kedgeree   *(English)*

An English adaptation of an old East Indian breakfast dish. English settlers also served it for lunch or supper.

2   cups cooked rice
1   lb. boiled fresh fish or
     canned or leftover fish
    salt and paprika

4   hard-boiled eggs, each cut in
     6 or 8 pieces
4   tbsp. butter
¼   cup cream

Mix together and heat in double boiler. Serve with crisp bacon.

Haddock Curls   *(English)*

4   tail-end pieces haddock fillets
    (about 3 oz. ea.)
1   tsp. lemon juice
2   tsp. seasoned flour
    cheese stuffing (see below)
1   egg, beaten

    raspings (crisp dried breadcrumbs)
1½ oz. butter
    lemon twists
    fresh parsley
1   cup cheese sauce (optional)

Wash, drain and dry fillets; sprinkle with lemon juice, then seasoned flour. Stuff each fillet with Cheese Stuffing, curl and tie. Brush with egg; dredge with raspings. Melt butter in baking tin. When hot, stand fish curls in pan and baste well. Bake in 350-375°F oven 20-25 minutes. Serve hot, garnished with lemon twists and parsley. Serve with cheese sauce, if desired.

Cheese Stuffing:

4   oz. Cheddar cheese, grated
2   oz. fresh bread crumbs
1   egg, beaten

1   tsp. salt
    cayenne pepper
1   tbsp. chopped parsley

Combine all ingredients.

Rabbit-In-Cider Casserole   (English)

1-2½ lb. rabbit, in serving-size pieces
⅓   cup butter
1¼   cups chopped onion
1   cup chopped carrots
⅓   cup broken walnuts

1   cup sliced mushrooms
2   tbsp. flour
1   tsp. salt
¼   tsp. pepper
1   cup apple cider

Brown rabbit in butter in large skillet. Transfer to 3-quart baking dish, reserving drippings in skillet. Add onion, carrots and nuts to drippings. Cook until vegetables are tender, not brown. Stir in mushrooms. Spoon mixture over rabbit, reserving drippings in skillet. Blend flour, salt and pepper into drippings; add cider and cook until thickened. Pour over meat and vegetables. Bake, covered, in 350°F oven 1 hour, or until done. Yield: 4-6 servings.

Veal and Ham Pie   (English)

pastry to cover sides and top
  of 1 lb. loaf tin
1   lb. veal fillets, cubed
6   oz. ham, cubed
     salt and pepper
½   tsp. grated lemon rind

1-2 hard-boiled eggs
7   tbsp. water or beef stock
1   egg, beaten (for glazing)
1   tsp. gelatin
½   tsp. meat extract

Line loaf tin with pastry. Roll cubed meats together in salt, pepper and lemon rind. Place half of meat on top of pastry. Cut eggs in half, place on meat and cover with remaining meat. Pour 3 tbsp. water or stock over meat. Roll out enough pastry to make a lid. Press down well all around edges to secure. Make hole in centre. Brush top with beaten egg, decorate with pastry leaves, brush again with egg. Bake in 375°F oven 2-2½ hours. Cool. Melt gelatin in remaining water or stock, stir in meat extract. When pie is cool and gelatin starts to set, pour into pie through hole. Serve when set.

Shepherd's Pie   (English)

4   large potatoes
     water or stock
½   cup hot milk
     flour
     salt and pepper

1   qt. cubed cold cooked mutton
2   cups diced, cold boiled potatoes
1   tbsp. butter
     milk

Boil 4 potatoes in water or stock, then mash with milk and enough flour to make a soft dough; season with salt and pepper. In baking dish, place a layer of half the diced mutton, a layer of half the diced potatoes, salt and pepper. Repeat layers. Cut butter into bits and dot on top. Pat out mashed potato mixture on slightly floured board, about size of baking dish. Place dough on top of pie; make a slight hole in middle and brush with a little milk. Bake in 350°F oven about 1 hour.

Pork Pie   (English)

Crust:

3 cups flour	¾ cup milk
1 tsp. salt	¾ cup lard

Sift flour and salt. Mix milk and lard in saucepan, and heat until lard melts. Add to flour and blend well. Knead on lightly floured board until smooth. Dough will be moist. Roll to ¼" thick. Cut a piece to line standard loaf pan, bottom and sides.

Filling:

1½ lb. pork shoulder, cubed	¼ tsp. sage
½ cup bread crumbs	¼ tsp. pepper
2 tsp. salt	1 cup stock

Combine above ingredients, except stock, and spoon into crust in loaf pan. Cover with remaining crust. Make several slashes in top crust. Bake in 325°F oven 1½ hours. Just before pie is done, heat stock. Remove pie from oven and carefully pour hot stock through slashes in crust. Let stand 10 minutes before serving.

Suggestion: Chill and serve cold. Slice in thick slices. Makes 6 to 8 servings.

Cold Pork Pie   (English)

3 lbs. lean pork shoulder, cubed	salt and pepper
1 veal knuckle*	pastry for 2-crust pie
2 onions, coarsely chopped	

Trim fat and gristle from pork, then cube. Place trimmings, with the fat, in pot with veal, 1 onion and seasoning to taste. Cover with water and slowly simmer 3 hours. Line an earthen casserole with pastry; fill ¾ full with pork cubes. Add second onion and seasonings. Pour in water to 1" deep. Put on top crust, seal edges, cut small hole in centre of top crust. Bake in 350°F oven 1½-3 hours. Tie thick brown paper over top if it gets too brown. Now broth should be cooked down to about 2 cups. Strain into pouring vessel, remove fat, and, using a funnel, pour into pork pie through hole in centre. Cool pie and chill until broth has gelled.

*If you can't get a veal knuckle, 1 tbsp. gelatin dissolved in 2 cups mild stock (chicken or dilute beef) would work.

Horseradish – Has been used for about 1000 years. In Britain, during the Middle Ages, it was used as a common medicine, but not eaten. It was considered a remedy for gout, whooping cough, worms, and used to get rid of freckles and bruises. Added to the bath, or in poultices, it was used for treatment of rheumatism and chilblains. In 16th century Germany, it was used in sauces for fish and meat.

Bubble and Squeak   (*English*)

1 lb. sausage meat, cooked	2 cups cream sauce, below
2 cups chopped cooked cabbage	bread crumbs

Layer meat and cabbage in casserole. Pour cream sauce over top and sprinkle with bread crumbs. Bake in 350°F oven 30 minutes. Serves 4-6.

Cream Sauce:

4 tbsp. butter	2 cups milk
4 tbsp. flour	salt and pepper

In double boiler or small saucepan melt butter, then stir in flour and blend well. Slowly add milk, stirring constantly; bring to a boil and cook 2-3 minutes. Season to taste. Makes 2 cups.

Eleanor's Yorkshire Pudding   (*English*)

3 eggs, beaten	1½ tsp. salt
5-6 tbsp. flour	1 cup milk

Prepare about 1 hour before you wish to start cooking it. To eggs, add flour and salt and beat well. Thoroughly mix in the milk. Refrigerate until you are ready to cook it. Beat again and pour batter into hot oil in 9" pan*. Bake in 400-450°F oven for 20 minutes. Reduce heat to 350°F and keep in oven until you serve it hot from the oven with the roast beef. Serves 6.

* *It was customary to cook this old and delicious dish in the roasting pan in a hot oven, but as we now cook roast in a slow oven, it is best to cook it separately. It will puff up and brown in a hot oven. When roast is cooked to your liking, heat oven to 400-450°F. Take roast out of oven and put hot fat from roast into a 9" pan, coating sides and bottom of pan, and keep hot. Add batter and cook as above.*

Corned Beef and Cabbage   (*Irish*)

corned beef	3 small cabbages, halved or 1 large
6 large onions, cut in large chunks	cabbage, cut in 6-8 wedges
6 large carrots, cut in thirds or quarters	with the some core on each
	6 potatoes, halved or quartered
	(optional)

In large pot cover corned beef with cold water. Bring to a boil, remove scum, reduce heat and simmer at least 5 hours. In last hour add onions and carrots. In last half-hour add cabbage and potatoes, if using. Carve corned beef in thin angled slices; serve hot. Drain vegetables, place in casserole and serve hot. Hot mustard and/or horseradish are a "must" with the corned beef.

Variation: Turnips may be added; also leeks can be used in place of onions.

Authentic Irish Stew   *(Irish)*

4   lbs. neck of mutton   12   potatoes, peeled
    salt and pepper   2   cups stock or water
8   medium to large onions

Divide the neck of mutton into 8-10 trimmed chops, paring away all excess fat and rough bone (a most necessary precaution). Season liberally with pepper and moderately with salt. Place chops in a deep saucepan with sufficient water to cover. Add onions and cook, covered, for ½ hour. Remove from heat and pour liquid into bowl. Remove all fat (essential!), then pour back on chops. Add potatoes and stock. Boil gently about ¼ hour.

To Serve: Place potatoes in the centre of a serving platter, arrange chops around them, pour sauce and onions over all. Serve very hot.

Mrs. Ings, at Midway ranch, Nanton, ca.1911

Golwythen O Borc *(Tenderloin of Pork)*   *(Welsh)*

1½ lbs. pork tenderloin (2 pieces)

Stuffing:

½   cup grated suet   salt and pepper
4   cups breadcrumbs   ⅔   cup cold cooked apples
8   oz. sausage meat   parsley, chopped
¾   cup water   ½-¾   cup raisins

Mix stuffing ingredients and spread on 1 piece of pork tenderloin. Place second tenderloin over filling. Tie in 3 or 4 places with string to hold together (to form a stuffed meat log). Bake in 350°F oven about 45 minutes.

Stovies   *(Scottish)*

drippings or fat
1 onion, sliced
several potatoes, peeled, sliced

salt and pepper
chopped leftover meat (if desired)

In a heavy skillet, heat drippings until smoking. Fry onion. Add potatoes and salt and pepper. Turn down heat, cover and simmer 1-2 hours (depending on amount of potatoes). When ready, stir up from bottom, and stir in meat. Heat and serve.

Note: The secret is to cook the potatoes without burning – and without lifting lid while cooking.

Haddock Fritters   *(Scottish)*

1 haddock
1 egg, hard-boiled
1 tsp. cream

1 tsp. butter
salt and pepper
parsley, finely chopped

Parboil haddock, bone, rub fish and egg through sieve. Place in bowl, add remaining ingredients and mix well. Make into small balls and dip in batter. Fry in hot fat until light brown.

Batter:

1½ tbsp. flour
water
1 tbsp. butter, melted

salt and pepper
1 egg white, lightly beaten

Mix flour with a little water to make a smooth paste. Add butter, seasoning and egg white, mixing lightly until well blended.

Haggis in a Pan   *(Scottish)*

½ lb. liver
1 large onion, parboiled
1 teacup oatmeal

¼ lb. chopped suet
seasoning
1 cup liquid

In a little water, boil the liver and onion 45 minutes. Pour off liquid and save. Chop onion. When liver is cold, grate and mix with onion. In a frying pan, brown oatmeal carefully, mix in liver, onion, suet and seasoning. Add a little liver liquid to moisten and simmer slowly 1½ hours, or steam in a greased pan 2 hours.

Atholl Brose   *(Scottish)*

2 parts honey
1 part whisky

6 parts cream

Mix honey and whisky together, stir in cream and ladle into glasses.

> *"The dish that he'll to supper teuk*
> *Was always Atholl Brose."*
>   - *Gaelic Verse*

Granny Hardwick's Mincemeat (Nov. 19, 1884)

This mincemeat has been kept in continuous use from year to year. After Christmas baking, leave a small amount in the crock and add the above ingredients to it in January. Let season through the year and repeat.

¼ lb. raisins
¼ lb. sultanas, chopped
¼ lb. currants
¼ lb. mixed peel, chopped
½ lb. apples, chopped

¼ lb. suet, chopped
¼ lb. moist sugar
1   tsp. mixed spices (nutmeg, mace, cinnamon)
½ cup brandy

Mix all ingredients well, except the brandy, put in earthenware jug, pour brandy over. Store.

Old-Fashioned Poundcake   (English)

1 lb. butter
1 lb. cake flour, sifted
10 eggs, separated

1 lb. sugar
1 tsp. vanilla

Cream the butter; work in the flour until mealy. Beat the egg yolks, vanilla and 1/2 of sugar until thick and lemon-coloured, then beat well into flour mixture. Beat egg whites until soft peaks form. Gradually beat in the rest of the sugar. Fold the whites into the batter; stir until blended. Pour into 2 greased and lined loaf pans. Bake at 325°F about 1¼ hours.

Ginger Cake   (English)

¾ cup butter
1 cup white sugar
1 cup brown sugar
2 eggs
3¾ cups flour

1 tsp. baking soda
1 tsp. nutmeg
1 cup sour milk
¾ cup chopped preserved ginger

Cream butter. Gradually add sugars, creaming well. Beat in eggs, 1 at a time. Combine 3½ cups flour with baking soda and nutmeg; add alternately with milk to creamed mixture. Toss remaining ¼ cup of flour with ginger; stir into batter. Spread evenly in 2 greased and floured 4 x 8" loaf pans or a 9" bundt pan. Bake in 350°F oven for 60-70 minutes for bundt pan or 45-55 minutes for loaf pans, or until done. Remove from pan(s) and let cool completely.

Wine Trifle   (English)

1⅔ cups rich milk
4   egg yolks, beaten slightly
¼   cup sugar
½   tsp. salt
½   tsp. vanilla
⅔   cup sherry, divided

1   sponge cake (see below)
⅓   cup raspberry or strawberry jam
20 ozs. fresh or preserved
        raspberries or strawberries
    whipping cream
⅓   cup almonds, toasted and split

Scald milk. Combine egg yolks, sugar and salt. Add milk to egg mixture and stir. Turn into double boiler and cook over hot water, stirring until mixture thickens and coats spoon. Add vanilla and ⅓ cup sherry. Beat well. Chill. Cut cake into 2 layers. Spread with some jam, top with second half of cake and more jam. Sprinkle remaining ⅓ cup sherry over cake. Pour chilled custard over cake. Chill several hours or overnight. To serve, whip the cream, put on top and sprinkle with nuts. Serves 6

Sponge Cake   (English)

1½ cups sifted flour
1   tsp. baking powder
⅛   tsp. salt
3   eggs, beaten

1   cup sugar
⅓   cup water
1   tsp. vanilla

Sift flour, baking powder and salt. Beat eggs until light and frothy. Gradually add sugar, beating until light coloured. Add water and vanilla. Fold in dry ingredients, blending well. Turn into (ungreased) springform pan. Bake in moderate oven (350°F) 25-35 minutes. Cool before removing from pan.

Pork Cake   (Irish)

    boiling water
½   cup raisins
½   cup currants
1   cup strong coffee
½   lb. salt pork, finely ground
1   cup brown sugar

1   egg, slightly beaten
½   cup molasses
3   cups flour
½   tsp. baking soda
1   tsp.each cinnamon, cloves
½   tsp. nutmeg

Pour boiling water over raisins and currants; let stand. Pour hot coffee over ground pork; let cool. Blend sugar, egg and molasses, then mix well into ground pork mixture. Drain raisins and currants. Sift dry ingredients, sprinkle over raisins and currants and stir to cover. Add to pork mixture and stir well. Grease fruitcake pan and line with brown paper, also greased, then pour in batter. Bake in 350°F oven 1½ hours, or until it tests done. Cool. When cool, wrap with cloth moistened with sherry. Store in cool place at least a week before serving.

Dundee Cake (*Scottish*)

3-6 oz. currants
6 oz. raisins
2 oz. glacé cherries
2 oz. mixed peel
8 oz. flour
1 tsp. baking powder

5 oz. butter
5 oz. caster sugar
3 eggs
2 tbsp. ground almonds
½ lemon, grated rind and juice of
split almonds

Line a round 7" cake tin* with greased paper. Prepare the fruit, sift flour and baking powder. Cream butter and sugar until light. Beat in eggs, one at a time, adding a small quantity of flour if the mixture shows a tendency to curdle. Stir in flour, ground almonds, fruit and lemon rind and juice. Turn into lined tin(s), make a depression in centre and arrange split almonds on top of cake. Bake in middle of 330°F oven for 1-1½ hours.

*An 8" tube cake tin, without paper, but greased, works fine.

Helen McCormick's Butterscotch Cake

2 cups brown sugar
¾ cup butter
¼ cup water
2 eggs, beaten
1½ cups bread flour

1 tsp. baking powder
1 cup walnuts
½ cup coconut
2 tsp. vanilla
1¼ tsp. salt

Boil the sugar, butter and water together for 2 minutes. Remove from stove and add remaining ingredients. Mix well and pour into greased cake pan. Bake 35 minutes at 350°F. Ice cake while still warm. This square is better if it is about 1½" thick.

Brown Sugar Icing:

1 cup brown sugar
3 tbsp. butter

5 tbsp. cream
icing sugar

Combine brown sugar, butter and cream. Boil together 5 minutes. Take from the stove and add icing sugar to stiffen, about 1 cup. Beat until it begins to thicken, and pour over the cake while warm.

Cacen Y Glowr (*Miner's Fruitcake*) (*Welsh*)

4 cups flour
  salt
1⅓ cups sugar
1 cup drippings or shortening
½ cup grated cheese

2½ cups mixed fruit (raisins,
  currants, cherries)
4 eggs, beaten
6-8 tbsp. milk

Sift dry ingredients into large bowl. Cut in drippings until blended and crumbly. Mix in cheese and fruit. Make a well and pour in the eggs and milk. Stir together just until blended. Place in greased loaf pan(s) and bake at 300°F 1¾ hours.

Barmbrack (Irish)

1 cup hot strong tea	1 egg, beaten
½ cup chopped dates	2 cups flour
½ cup chopped mixed peel	1 tsp. baking powder
1 cup washed raisins	¼ tsp. baking soda
1 cup brown sugar	¼ tsp. salt

Pour tea over fruit and sugar; let stand overnight. Next morning stir in egg, then sifted dry ingredients. Turn into greased loaf pan and bake for 1½ hours at 300°F. Turn onto wire rack to cool. To serve, slice and butter.

Bachelor's Buttons (Irish)

¾ cup butter	1 tsp. baking soda
¾ cup brown sugar	½ cup coconut
1 egg	½ cup slivered almonds
½ tsp. vanilla	½ cup chopped cherries
1¾ cups flour, sifted	

Cream butter and sugar, drop in egg and beat. Add vanilla. Sift flour and baking soda. Add to sugar mixture. Stir in coconut, almonds and cherries. Mix by hand, shape into small balls, place on ungreased cookie sheet. Bake in 375°F oven about 10 minutes. Yield: about 4 dozen cookies

Note: Whole-wheat flour may be used, but sift out most of the bran.

Vanilla – Native to Central America and Mexico, it has a distinct but subtle sweet flavor. Aztecs enjoyed a drink made with cocoa and vanilla beans "Xoco–Latl", they also developed a way to cure beans without losing flavor. The vanilla bean was later discovered by Cortez, taken to Spain and then to Europe. It is third most expensive spice after Saffron and Cardomom. The best quality vanilla is from Vera Cruz and Mexico. The first artificial vanilla was produced in 1974 because of the expense of vanilla beans. 90% of the vanilla used now is artificial.

Uses: hot and cold beverages, puddings, cakes, cookies, desserts, stewed fruits, pastry fillings, breads.

Chocolate – "Food of the Gods", in 1500s, when Cortez conquered Mexico, the Aztecs were already using a drink "chocolatl" – made from the beans of the cacao tree. It was the preferred beverage of the ruling or upper classes in ancient Guatemala.

Cottage Dumpling (Scottish)

Sally Erdman's grandmother, Mrs. Elizabeth (Richard) Urch, came to a log ranch house near Fort Kipp on the Oldman River, from Gloucestershire. Sally remembers her wonderful meals and her Apple (Fruit) and Cottage Dumplings.

½ lb. flour
¼ lb. breadcrumbs
6 oz. suet, ground or chopped
¼ lb. currants
½ lb. dates, chopped

¼ tsp. baking soda
1 tsp. each cinnamon, ginger, mixed spices
1 teacup marmalade
milk

Mix all the ingredients, adding marmalade second last, then stir in enough milk to make a soft dough. Scald a pudding cloth, sprinkle with flour, place pudding dough in cloth and tie firmly, leaving enough room for dough to expand. Boil for 3½ hours. Turn onto platter and serve with a favorite sauce.

Grannie Urch's Plum Pudding (Scottish)

3 oz. flour
3 oz. bread crumbs
¾ lb. fruit (raisins, currants)
6 oz. suet, ground or chopped
5 oz. sugar
½ cup molasses

1½ oz. peel
½ tsp. nutmeg
½ tsp. mace
1 tsp. salt
3 eggs
beer, enough to moisten

Mix all the ingredients and let stand 1 hour. Put in a greased bowl, cover with waxed paper and steam about 3-4 hours.

Fruit Roll (Scottish)

A traditional Scottish recipe.

2 cups flour
¾ tsp. salt
4 tsp. baking powder
2 tbsp. shortening
¾ cup milk

1 tbsp. butter, melted
2 cups finely chopped apples
¼ cup raisins
1 tbsp. sugar
1 tsp. cinnamon

Sift flour, salt and baking powder; rub in shortening. Mix to a light dough with milk. Roll to ¼" thick. Brush dough with melted butter. Mix together apples, raisins, sugar and cinnamon and sprinkle on buttered dough. Roll up dough, moisten edges and pinch together. Place in greased dish, combine topping ingredients, below, and pour over the roll. Bake in 350°F oven 35-40 minutes, basting frequently with molasses mixture.

Molasses Topping:
¾ cup molasses
1 cup water

2 tbsp. butter
¼ tsp. nutmeg

Mix together and pour over roll.

Congregational Crumble (Scottish)

Because it is made from offerings of seasonal fruit supplied by the Congregation.

2 lbs. prepared fruit (plums, apples, blackberries, raspberries, etc.)	8 oz. flour
8 oz. brown sugar	4 oz. porridge oats
4 oz. butter	2 tsp. cinnamon

Put harder fruits in a pan and add half of sugar, cook over low heat until barely tender, then add softer fruits. Turn into a greased 2-quart dish. Rub butter into flour, add remaining half of sugar, oats, and cinnamon, then mix until crumbly. Spoon mixture over fruit and press down lightly. Bake in 375-400°F oven about 30 minutes. Serve hot or cold, with pouring cream.

Margaret's Carrot Pudding (Scottish)

1 cup grated carrot	½ cup bread crumbs
1 cup grated potato	½ tsp. salt
1 cup chopped or ground suet	1½ cups flour
1 cup brown sugar	1 tsp. cinnamon
1 cup raisins	1 tsp. nutmeg
1 cup chopped figs	¼ tsp. cloves
½ cup currants	¼ tsp. mace
½ cup peel	1 tsp. baking soda
½ cup cherries	

Mix all together and pat into 2 moulds. Steam 3 hours. Serve warm. Can be made ahead and stored in a cool place. Steam 1-2 hours again before serving. Serve with Sterling Sauce, below, Hard Sauce or your favourite pudding sauce.

Sterling Sauce

3 tbsp. butter, or less	½ tbsp. cream or milk
4 heaping tbsp. brown sugar	½ tsp. vanilla

Combine in order given in top of double boiler. Add sugar and milk together. Heat but don't let it get too hot. Can be kept warm in double boiler. Stir occasionally. Serve with or on Margaret's Carrot Pudding, above.

Pwdin Mynwy (Monmouth Pudding) (Welsh)

1¾ cups milk	4 egg yolks, slightly beaten
2 lemons, grated, rind of	4 cups fresh breadcrumbs
2 oz. sugar	red jam
1½ oz. butter	

In saucepan combine first 4 ingredients. Bring to a boil, then cool. Stir in yolks; pour over breadcrumbs and mix. Pour half of the mixture in a greased casserole, spread jam over, then pour in remaining mixture. Bake at 300°F, ¾ hour, until set.

SCANDINAVIAN

Mrs. E.P. Oveson, at cookhouse, on farm, Floram area, ca. 1914

Scandinavian Immigrants

A group of immigrants from Iceland settled in Gimli, Manitoba in 1872. From there they spread across the Prairies, usually as farmers. Although the smallest of the Scandinavian groups, they have retained the strongest ethnic identity.

Stephan Stephansson immigrated to North America in 1873, to Wisconsin, and then North Dakota. He settled in Markerville, Alberta in 1889. He homesteaded, and also authored 6 large books of poetry and scores of articles in Iceland.

Scandinavians were fleeing a system of tenant farming and crop failures.

They came to the New World to escape poverty. The U.S.A. received nearly all the immigrants, but as the frontier in the U.S. receded, Canada became the "Land of another chance". These people had already learned frontier skills and they did well in western Canada.

The first Norwegian settlement in Alberta was at Calgary when the Eau Claire Lumber Co. was established in 1886.

An' Da Lefse

An' now hyar's a plate off lefse
  Dat vil naver go tew vaste . . .
It iss used at all da smorgasbords
  Cause it sharpen oop da taste.
Maybe som vill t'ink dey're napkins
  For tew cover oop deir shirt . . .
Men da lefse means at smorgasbords
  Dey vill gat deir moneys' vort' . .

Lefse (Potato Treats)   (Norwegian)

2 cups potatoes
4 tbsp. butter

milk or cream
2 cups flour

Cook and mash potatoes. Add butter and a little milk; beat until fluffy. Mix in flour to make a dough. On a lightly floured board, roll out dough as thin as possible, in several small circles, 8" in diameter. Fry one at a time on griddle until lightly browned. Before each frying, grease griddle by wiping with a cloth dipped in a little oil. Remove cooked Lefse from pan, cover with a towel until cool. Spread with butter, sprinkle with sugar, roll like a jelly roll and cut in 3-4" lengths.

Julekage (Christmas Bread) (Danish)

1 pkg. dry yeast	4 cups flour
¼ cup warm milk	1 cup milk
½ cup butter	1 egg, lightly beaten
¼ cup sugar	½ cup raisins
1 tsp. salt	½ cup candied fruit

In a large bowl, dissolve the yeast in warm milk. Mix in the butter, sugar and salt. Sift flour onto mixture; add remaining ingredients. Mix well, and knead dough until springy and elastic. Place in a greased bowl, set in a warm place and let rise about 2 hours, until double in size. Knead lightly on lightly floured board, form into loaves and place in well-greased loaf pans. Cover, let rise again to double in size, about 1 hour. Prior to baking, brush with a lightly beaten egg to add shine to bread. Bake in 350°F oven 30-35 minutes. When baked, ice with a mixture of powdered sugar and a little water drizzled over the loaves.

Ponnukokur (Pancakes) (Icelandic)

These have a crêpe-like texture. They are traditionally served with hot chocolate on Christmas Eve.

2 eggs	½ tsp. baking soda
⅓ cup sugar	½ cup sour cream or buttermilk
¼ tsp. salt	1½ cups flour
½ tsp. vanilla	1 tsp. baking powder
½ tsp. cinnamon	2 cups sweet milk

Beat eggs. Add sugar, salt, vanilla and cinnamon. Dissolve baking soda in a little boiling water and mix with the sour cream or buttermilk. Add to egg and sugar mixture. Add flour sifted with the baking powder and beat well. Gradually stir in the sweet milk. Heat buttered griddle. For each pancake, lift griddle off heat and pour about ⅕ cup of batter on it, tilting griddle until the bottom is completely covered with batter. Return to heat as quickly as possible. Brown lightly, then flip over and brown second side lightly as well. Turn out on a large flat dish. Sprinkle with sugar and roll up.

Pannekaker *(Pancakes)* *(Norwegian)*

1 cup + 2 tbsp. flour
½ tsp. salt
¼ tsp. cardamom
3 egg yolks
1 cup milk

3 egg whites, stiffly beaten
melted butter
2 tbsp. powdered sugar
1½ cups blueberries, raspberries,
    fresh or stewed

Sift the first 3 ingredients. Beat egg yolks with milk and slowly stir in flour mixture until smooth. Fold in egg whites. Heat griddle; lightly coat with butter when hot. Drop pancake batter to a 3" diameter onto hot griddle, brown both sides, remove to cookie sheet and keep warm in oven. When all the pancakes are ready, sprinkle each with powdered sugar, place berries on half and fold over. For toppings, use sour cream or your favourite liqueur.

Knechebrod *(Thin Bread)* *(Norwegian)*

3 cups potato water
2 tbsp. yeast, dissolved in warm water
1 cup shortening
½ cup sweet cream

1 egg yolk
1 tbsp. salt
3 tbsp. sugar
flour

Mix all together, adding enough flour to make a soft dough. Knead down once, let rise, make into large buns. Set aside and let rise again, 1½-2 hours. Roll as thin as possible with notched rolling pin. Bake in hot (500°F) oven on bottom rack until barely brown, then move to upper rack to brown.

Brod *(Flat Bread)* *(Norwegian)*

1 cup graham flour
1 cup cornmeal
⅓ cup lard or shortening

1 tsp. salt
2 cups boiling water
1 cup white flour

Put graham flour, cornmeal, shortening and salt in a pan, pour boiling water over it and mix with a spoon. Let it stand until it cools, then mix with white flour. Do not knead. Roll out at once, very thin. Bake on the top of the stove. Dry in the oven at 250-300°F. Handle the rolled flat bread with a lefse turner – similar to a spatula and made of wood.

Rye Bread   *(Swedish)*

2 yeast cakes	½ cup molasses
1 tbsp. salt	1 cup dark corn syrup
1 cup water	7 cups rye flour, sifted
1 cup mashed potatoes	1 cup whole-wheat flour
3 cups warm potato water	1 cup soy flour
white flour	

Mix first 5 ingredients, stirring until yeast cakes dissolve. Thicken with some flour. Add molasses and syrup. Mix in flours, adding enough white flour to make a stiff dough. Knead well; let rise in warm place. Knead again. Let rise once more, then form into 6 or 7 loaves. Bake in 350°F oven for 1 hour.

Rarakor *(Potato Pancakes)*   *(Swedish)*

4 large potatoes, peeled	flour (if needed to thicken
3 tbsp. minced chives	mixture slightly)
1½ tsp. salt	2 tbsp. butter
⅛ tsp. pepper	2 tbsp. vegetable oil

In a bowl, cover potatoes with ice water. Drain and grate potatoes quickly; dry some of the moisture out with paper towel. Mix in chives, salt and pepper. Sprinkle in flour if needed. Put butter and oil in a large skillet over high heat. When hot, drop in about 2 tbsp. of mixture for each pancake; press flat with a spatula. Fry until golden and crisp, turning only once. Keep hot in 300°F oven.

Plattar *(Pancakes)*   *(Swedish)*

1¼ cups flour	3 eggs, beaten until fluffy
1 tsp. salt	melted butter for griddle
1 cup milk, divided	1 cup lingonberry or cranberry
2½ tbsp. melted butter	preserves, warmed

Sift together flour and salt. Add ¼ cup milk and melted butter to beaten eggs and beat well. To egg mixture, beat in remaining milk and flour, alternately. When smooth, cover and set aside for 1 hour. Heat a Swedish "plattlaj' (cast-iron griddle with 7 compartments for individual pancakes), or a heavy griddle. Thinly coat with butter. Beat batter once again, then pour about 1½ tbsp. per pancake on hot griddle, browning both sides. Spread with warm berries and serve.

Limpa *(Rye and Molasses Bread)* (*Swedish*)

This delicious Swedish bread has almost the same consistency as cake.

1 qt. ale	1 qt. molasses
2 lbs. rye flour	2 tbsp. chopped fennel
2 qts. milk	3 tbsp. chopped orange peel
3½ oz. yeast	⅞ cup butter
6 lbs. white flour	

Warm the ale, add to rye flour in large bowl. Work (stir) 15 minutes then let stand 12 hours. Stir in lukewarm milk with dissolved yeast and white flour. Set aside until dough has doubled original volume. Work in molasses, fennel, peel and enough white flour to make dough very stiff. Let rise until doubled. Shape into loaves; put these on a cloth in a warm place to rise. When well risen, brush tops with cold water and bake in warm oven about 40 minutes. Brush twice with cold water during baking and again when removed from oven.

Erikson family and friends, outside sod home, Veteran area, 1910

Glogg (*Swedish*)

Served as part of Swedish Christmas festivities and a sign of warm hospitality. Make a few days in advance.

3 cinnamon sticks	1 bottle domestic brandy
10 whole cloves	1 cup sugar
6 cardamom seeds	⅓ cup seedless raisins
1 glass red wine	few almonds, blanched
	chopped peel

Heat spices in enough wine to cover. Simmer gently 15 minutes. Add remaining ingredients. Bottle and seal tightly. To serve, heat, but do not boil, and add a few raisins, almonds and some chopped peel. Serve hot.

Ham and Bean Soup   *(Scandinavian)*

½ lb. kidney beans
2 qts. water
   smoked ham shank
1 onion, chopped
6 cloves

6 peppercorns
½ cup sugar
1 tbsp. vinegar
   bread crumbs (see below)

Cover the beans with water and soak overnight. Drain the next day. In a kettle place the 2 quarts of water, beans, ham shank, onion and spices. Simmer 3 hours. Remove bone and meat, then rub the rest through a strainer and put back in kettle. Add sugar and vinegar to taste, cut meat into small pieces and add to soup. Serve hot, sprinkled with bread crumbs.

Toasted Bread Crumbs:
2 tbsp. butter
1 tbsp. sugar

bread crumbs

In a frying pan, melt butter and blend with sugar. Add bread crumbs, stir until browned, then sprinkle over or serve with the soup.

Arter Och Flask *(Split Pea Soup)*   *(Swedish)*

National dish of Sweden for about 500 years; traditionally served on Thursday.

1   lb. dried yellow peas
3   qts. cold water
1½-2 lbs. lean pork (meat and bone)
1   onion, quartered

3 tsp. salt
1 bay leaf
4 whole peppercorns

In a large kettle, cover the peas with the water and soak overnight. Next day, place kettle over low heat, cooking the peas in same water. Stir occasionally during first hour. If using whole peas, skim off skins as they come to surface. When soup boils, add meat, bone, onion and seasonings. Cover and simmer 4 hours, stirring occasionally. Remove from heat; remove meat, bone and bay leaf. Set aside until ready to serve. (May be made the day before.) Reheat to serve.

Note: Meat can be served separately.

Asparagus – A favorite vegetable of the Ancient Greeks, it grows very quickly – like Jack's beanstock – up to 8-10" a day. The warmer the weather, the faster it grows; the faster it grows, the better it tastes!

Frukt Suppe *(Fruit Soup)* *(Norwegian)*

½ cup quick-cooking tapioca
3 cups water
½ cup raisins, cooked

½ cup pitted prunes, cooked
1 lemon, juice of
  sugar

In saucepan place water and tapioca, cooking tapioca until transparent. Add remaining ingredients, sweeten to taste. Simmer over low heat 3 or 4 minutes. Serve hot or cold.

Fish Chowder

3 cups water
3 potatoes, cubed
3 green onions with tops, in ½" pieces
1 bay leaf
¼ lb. boneless fish fillet (salmon, whitefish, trout), cubed

¾ cup heavy cream
2 tbsp. flour
1 tbsp. butter
1 tsp. salt
¼ tsp. pepper
  allspice

Bring water to a boil, add potatoes, onions and bay leaf. Reduce heat and simmer 20 minutes, until potatoes are tender. Stir in fish, cover and simmer 5 minutes Remove bay leaf. Mix cream and flour; stir gently into soup. Cover and simmer 5 more minutes, until soup thickens and the fish is cooked. Stir in butter, salt, pepper and a dash of allspice. Serves 4.

Suggestion: If using leftover baked or poached fish, add with butter and seasonings. Heat through, and serve.

Spinatsuppe *(Spinach Soup)* *(Norwegian)*

2 lbs. fresh spinach
2 qts. chicken stock
3 tbsp. butter
2 tbsp. flour

⅛ tsp. nutmeg
1 tsp. salt
  white pepper
2-3 eggs, hard-boiled, sliced

Wash and drain spinach, then coarsely chop. Bring chicken stock to boil, add spinach, then simmer, uncovered, about 6 minutes. Pour all into a sieve over a large bowl. Press down on spinach to remove all juices. Set liquid aside. Chop spinach very fine and set aside. In soup pot melt butter, add flour and mix well. Stir in the hot stock a little at a time. Heat, stirring constantly, and bring to boil. Add spinach, nutmeg, salt and pepper to taste. Partially cover pan and simmer over low heat 5 minutes, stirring occasionally. To serve, garnish each bowl with slices of hard-boiled eggs. Yield: 4-6 servings

Kesakeitto *(Summer Vegetable Soup)* *(Finnish)*

1½ cups diced carrots
⅔ cup fresh green peas
1 cup 1/2" cauliflower florets
½ cup diced potatoes
½ cup fresh stringbeans, cut in ¼" strips
4 small radishes, halved
¼ lb. fresh spinach, washed, finely chopped
2 tsp. salt
2 tbsp. butter

2 tbsp. flour
1 cup milk
1 egg yolk
¼ cup heavy cream
½ lb. medium cooked shrimp (optional)
¼ tsp. white pepper
2 tbsp. finely chopped fresh parsley or dillweed

Place all the vegetables, except the spinach, in a 3-quart pot, cover with cold water, add salt. Boil 5 minutes, or until vegetables are almost tender. Add spinach and cook 5 more minutes. Strain and set vegetables and stock in separate bowls. Melt butter, remove from heat, stir in flour. Slowly pour in hot stock, beating vigorously, then beat in milk. Combine egg yolk and cream; add a little hot stock, then add warm egg mixture to the stock. Stir well. Simmer 5 minutes. Add vegetables and heat. Season to taste. To serve, sprinkle with parsley and/or dill. Yield: 6 servings

Mr. and Mrs. Lokken, Viking area, 1918

Aggekage (Pancakes)　　　　　　(Danish)

½ lb. lean bacon slices or ham strips,
　　cut in halves
6 eggs
½ cup milk

½ tsp. salt
2 tbsp. flour
2 tbsp. chopped chives

In heavy skillet, cook bacon until crisp, drain on paper towel, keep warm in oven. Drain all but 2 tbsp. of bacon grease from pan. Beat eggs until fluffy, beat in milk and salt and sprinkle in flour. Reheat pan with reserved bacon grease, pour in all the batter to cover entire surface. Turn heat to low, cook until batter is firm about 15-20 minutes, like a custard, then sprinkle with chives and bacon slices. Cut in wedges and serve hot.

Appel-Flask (Bacon with Apple and Onion Rings) (Swedish)

2 tbsp. butter
1 lb. back bacon
2 large onions, sliced fairly thin

2 large, tart red apples, unpeeled,
　　cored, cut in ½" rings
black peppercorns

Melt butter; fry bacon until lightly browned. Remove from pan. Fry onion slices until translucent, adding more butter if necessary, then add apple rings and cover pan. Simmer about 8 minutes, shaking pan gently to prevent sticking. Add bacon and simmer 3-5 minutes, until bacon is heated through. Grind pepper liberally over top and serve directly from pan. Yield: 4 servings

Citrus Fruits – Grown in India and China 2000 years ago, citrus fruits were used by ancient Greeks in medicines and cooking. Oranges brought to Europe by Crusaders, were believed native to South China and Burma. In the 17th Century the Spanish took oranges to the Americas – planted in Florida, California and South America. Lemons were brought from the Middle East to Spain and North Africa during the Middle Ages. Native to India, their cultivation dates back 2500 years. Grapefruits, cultivated for about 2000 years in India and Malaysia, were introduced to America in the 19th Century.

Kalvsylta (Jellied Veal)   (Scandinavian)

1 veal shank or knuckle	seasonings of choice
2 qts. water	pinch of ginger
1 tsp. peppercorns	¼ cup vinegar
1 tbsp. salt	

Add veal to water and bring to a boil. Skim off fat, then add peppercorns, salt and seasonings of choice. Cook until meat is tender. Remove meat and cool. Continue cooking broth. Chop meat fine and place in mould. Strain broth, add ginger and vinegar, then season to taste. Pour over meat, chill and let set overnight. Remove from mould and serve.

Paistetut Sienet (Mushrooms in Heavy Cream) (Finnish)

¼ cup finely chopped onions	¼ cup dry bread crumbs
4 tbsp. butter	½ cup heavy cream
1 lb. mushrooms, thinly sliced	salt and pepper

Sauté onions in butter until transparent; add mushrooms and cook another 3-5 minutes, stirring often. When mushrooms are light brown, add breadcrumbs and stir gently with wooden spoon. Remove from heat. Beat the cream with a whisk about 2 minutes, add to mushrooms, toss lightly until the mushrooms are well coated, add salt and pepper. Yield: 4 servings.

Suggestion: Serve with meat or fish dishes.

Skyr (Skim Milk)   (Icelandic)

1 gal. fresh skim milk	1 cup cultured buttermilk

Bring milk to boil. Cool to lukewarm (75-85°F). Add buttermilk, stir, let stand 12-15 hours at room temperature (above 72°F). Line a bowl or pot with fine cheesecloth, pour in milk. Lift cloth by 4 corners and hang to drain at warm room temperature 12 hours. Chill. Keeps 2 weeks. Can be eaten plain or with sugar, and used on porridge instead of milk.

Note: The difference between Skyr and Yogurt is that Skyr cultures between 72 and 85°F. It will not culture below 72°F. Yogurt cultures at about 105°F.

Honey – Made from the nectar of flowers, it has been used in cooking since ancient times. By the Bronze Age domesticated beekeeping was widespread. Honey is still popular today. You need less honey than sugar when cooking.

Scalloped Potato Casserole   (*Finnish*)
with Salt Pork and Herring

5	medium potatoes, thinly sliced	¼	lb. salt pork, in small pieces
	salt and pepper	1	salt herring, in small pieces
2	tbsp. flour		water
4	tbsp. butter		

In a buttered casserole, place layer of potatoes, salt and pepper, a little flour, dabs of butter, and a few pieces of pork. For the next layer, do the same, except use pieces of herring. Repeat until all ingredients are used; the top layer is a thin layer of potatoes. Add water until it can be seen in the potatoes. Cover, bake in 350°F oven 1-1½ hours, or until potatoes are tender. To brown top, remove cover for last 15 minutes. Yield: 5 or 6 servings.

Baked Pike   (*Finnish*)

3-3½	lbs. whole pike	2	eggs, hard-boiled, chopped
3	qts. boiling salted water	½	cup finely chopped parsley
⅔	cup rice	¼	cup finely chopped chives
1	large cucumber, peeled, seeded, coarsely chopped*	⅛	tsp. pepper
		1-3	tbsp. cream
1¼	tsp. salt	¼	lb. butter
½	cup finely chopped onions	6	tbsp. dry bread crumbs
2	tbsp. butter	½	cup boiling water

Clean, scale** and remove backbone from pike, leave head and tail on. Cook rice until slightly firm, about 12 minutes, drain and set aside. In small bowl toss cucumber with ¼ tsp. salt, let stand 15 minutes, then drain and pat dry. Cook cucumber and onions until translucent, in 2 tbsp. butter – do not brown. Place in a large bowl and add eggs, rice, parsley, chives, 1 tsp. salt and pepper. Moisten with cream. Mix lightly but thoroughly. Dry inside of fish well, fill with stuffing, weave opening closed with skewers and string. In baking dish suitable for serving, melt ¼ lb. butter on medium heat. Cook fish until golden brown, about 5 minutes, carefully turn and brown other side. Sprinkle with breadcrumbs, turn again, and sprinkle with more crumbs. Pour ½ cup boiling water around fish and bring to simmer on top of stove, then bake, uncovered, in 350°F oven 30-35 minutes, until fish feels firm. Serve from baking dish. Yield: 4-6 servings.

* 1 cup finely chopped and cooked spinach, squeezed dry, can be used instead of cucumber.

** *To Scale Fish:* Pour white vinegar over fish, scrape with a dull knife and scales come off easily. Generously sprinkle freshly caught fish with salt, then wrap in vinegar-soaked cloth before bringing catch home from the favourite fishing spot – it won't smell so "fishy"!

Be sure to serve crisp bacon with trout. They go hand in hand, like bacon and eggs.

Fiskeboller (Fish Balls)   (Norwegian)

2   qts. whole milk
2   dozen fresh herring or blue fins
4   small raw potatoes, peeled
⅓   cup soft butter

3   eggs, well beaten
¼   tsp. each mace and nutmeg
    salt and pepper to taste

Scald milk and chill. Scale fish and remove skin and bones. Put bones and skin in kettle and add enough salted water to cover. Boil 10 minutes, strain liquid to fill a kettle ½ full. Use liquid to boil fish balls. Grind scraped fish through a meat grinder with raw potatoes, 3-5 times. Put in a bowl and with the help of a wooden potato masher use a pounding and mashing effect on ground fish until it forms a tough dough. Add soft butter and continue mashing; add beaten eggs and chilled milk, 1 cup at a time, with much pounding and mashing in between. Add spices and seasoning to taste. Bring the fish stock back to a boil. When fish mixture is light and fluffy, dip a tablespoon in cold water, then into the fish batter; drop into boiling fish broth. Let boil 7-8 minutes, until dumplings rise to the surface. Put dumplings in earthen crock and pour fish stock over. This will keep 6 weeks in a cool place or it can be put in sealers.

To Serve: Fry in butter until delicately browned or make a white sauce to pour over.

Fish Pudding   (Norwegian)

2   lbs. white fish, finely chopped
¼   cup butter
½   cup cream
    salt and pepper

2   eggs, beaten
2   tbsp. flour
⅛   tsp. nutmeg

Combine all ingredients and beat until light. Pour into greased mould and set in pan of hot water. Bake in moderate (350°F) oven about 1 hour, or until firm. Serve hot.

Rulle Polse   (Norwegian)

Prepare a veal or beef flank. If not meaty add extra strips of meat and a few strips of bacon. Sprinkle with salt, pepper, ginger and some finely chopped onion to taste. Roll up like a jelly roll and tie with strong string. Wrap well with cord (cloth if you wish) before boiling for about ½ hour. Put into a press until cold. Put into brine 4-5 days before using. This makes excellent cold meat.

Farsrulader (Veal Roulades)   (Swedish)

1	medium potato, quartered	½	tsp. pepper
2	tbsp. butter	1	egg, lightly beaten
¼	cup finely chopped onion	2	tbsp. finely chopped parsley
1	lb. veal, finely ground	1	tbsp. cornstarch
3	tbsp. fine bread crumbs	½	cup thin slices of leeks,
⅓	cup heavy cream		white part only
2	tbsp. water	¼	lb. butter
1½	tsp. salt	¼	cup heavy cream

Boil potato until tender, drain, mash with fork. In 2 tbsp. butter, sauté onions until translucent, not brown. Mix onions in bowl with potato, veal, bread crumbs ⅓ cup heavy cream, water, salt, pepper, egg, parsley and cornstarch. Mix well and chill 1 hour. Brush water on large board or hard surface, roll out meat mixture to a 16" square, about ⅛" thick. Moisten hands to prevent sticking. Cut meat into 16, 4" squares. Place leek slices on each square, then roll each square, jelly-roll fashion. Chill 1 hour. Brown rolls in melted butter, turning gently until well browned and cooked. Set aside in 200°F oven. Pour ¼ cup heavy cream into drippings, boil 3-5 minutes until thickened; season to taste and pour over roulades and serve. Yield: 16 roulades.

Kottbullar (Meat Balls)   (Swedish)

½	lb. beef, minced	½	cup breadcrumbs
¼	lb. veal, minced	2	tbsp. finely chopped onion
¼	lb. pork, minced		salt and pepper to taste
1-2	eggs	4	tbsp. butter
2-3	cups milk	1	cup boiling water

Put meat through grinder 3 times. Beat eggs with milk, add breadcrumbs and let soak until they swell. Fry chopped onions to a golden brown. Mix meat with breadcrumb mixture; add onion, salt and pepper. Shape into small balls; fry in butter. When brown, add boiling water, simmer 15 minutes and serve hot. Yield: 6 servings.

The smorgasbord is almost a national institution in Sweden. A number of small dishes containing all manner of delicacies – anchovies, smoked salmon, herring in vinegar, herring salad, various kinds of sliced meats – are placed on a side table and eaten with bread and butter and a glass of spirits.

Potato Sausage (1914) *(Swedish)*

1 medium onion
6 raw potatoes
2½ lbs. ground pork
½ lb. ground beef
1 tsp. pepper

3 tbsp. salt
¾ tsp. allspice
2 tsp. ginger
1 cup milk, scalded
1 lb. casings

Grind onion and potatoes, then mix with ground meats. Add spices, milk and mix thoroughly, then stuff into casings. Allow space for expansion, so casings do not break when cooking. Bring to a boil in a large pot of water, turn down heat and simmer about 1 hour. Prick a couple of times during cooking.

Flaskkarre *(Loin of Pork)* *(Swedish)*

3 lb. loin of pork
15 dried prunes, pitted
12 dried apricots, pitted

1½ cups water
1 tsp. salt
¼ tsp. pepper

Remove visible fat from pork. With sharp knife, make slits lengthwise on roast, then rub with salt and pepper. Cover prunes with some water and bring to boil. Turn off heat, add apricots. Cool, then drain and save liquid. Insert half of prunes and apricots into slits. Tie meat up into a roast, place in a roasting pan and add 1 cup water. (Additional water may be added during cooking to prevent drying.) Bake in 325°F oven 1½-1¾ hours. (Do not overcook but leave no pink.) Yield: 6-8 servings.

Prune Apricot Sauce:

2 reserved fruit and juice from prunes and apricots above
1 cup dry white wine

1 cup chicken stock
pan drippings

In a small saucepan, mix all of above, bring to a simmer and cook 5 minutes. Purée until smooth, then return to pan and bring to a simmer. Serve over hot pork.

Optional: Thicken sauce with 1 tbsp. cornstarch mixed with 2 tbsp. water.

Onion – Native to W. Asia, it has a distinct aroma, and varies in taste from sharp to subtle. Known for over 4000 years; grown by the ancient Babylonians, it was eaten by Egyptian slaves building the pyramids. Available in powder, salt, minced, flakes, shredded, juice.

Uses: appetizers, soups, dips, sauces, stews, meats, poultry, fish, stuffing, cheese and egg dishes, breads, casseroles, salads.

Foedseldagskringle *(Birthday Cake)* *(Danish)*

3 pkgs. yeast
¼ cup warm water
¾ cup sugar
3 cups flour
½ cup milk

2 eggs, beaten
⅓ cup soft butter (not melted)
½ cup chopped nuts
   chopped candied fruit peel
1 egg, beaten
   sugar

Dissolve yeast in warm water. Sift sugar and flour, and add yeast, water, milk and first 2 eggs. Work dough well, set in warm place and let rise. On lightly floured board roll dough into 6 x 12" rectangle. Spread with butter, sprinkle with most of nuts and fruit. Fold each side to the middle so they overlap a little, pinch the seam closed. Shape into a ring, place on greased cookie sheet and let rise. Brush with a single beaten egg, sprinkle with sugar and remaining nuts. Bake in 350°F oven 45-50 minutes.

Brune Kager *(Brown or Spice Cookies)* *(Danish)*

These are traditional Christmas Cookies.

1 cup butter
¾ cup sugar
½ cup corn syrup
1 egg, lightly beaten
2¾ cups flour

1 tbsp. cinnamon
2 tsp. each ginger, cloves
1 tsp. baking soda
1 cup chopped nuts

Cream butter and sugar, stir in syrup and egg. Sift dry ingredients, mix in nuts and stir slowly into butter mixture with wooden spoon. Dough should be soft, not sticky. Divide dough into 4 pieces. On lightly floured board roll each piece into a log about 1½" diameter. Wrap and chill. When ready to bake, cut rolls in ¼" slices. Place on greased cookie sheet, leaving a little space between as they may spread a little. Bake in hot (375-400°F) oven 8-10 minutes, until golden brown. Yield: about 8 dozen cookies.

Genuine Kleiner (Doughnuts)　(Danish)

3 eggs, beaten
1 cup sugar
4 tbsp. cream
½ cup butter, melted
1 tsp. vanilla
1 tsp. cinnamon

¼ tsp. nutmeg
½ tsp. salt
1 tsp. baking powder
3-4 cups flour
1½ lbs. fat or 3 cups oil for frying

Cream eggs and sugar, blend in cream, butter, vanilla, spices, salt, baking powder and enough flour to make batter stiff enough to roll out like cookies. Cut in diamond shapes, make slit in centre and pull one end through slit. Cook 6-8 at a time in deep hot fat or oil until light brown, turning with fork*. Place on brown paper to cool.

* A metal knitting needle may work better than a fork.

Weinerbrod (Danish Pastry)

1 pkg. yeast
¼ cup warm water
1 cup cold milk
1 egg
10 cardamom seeds

1½ tbsp. sugar
½ tsp. salt
3 cups flour
1 cup softened butter

Sprinkle yeast over warm water and let stand 10 minutes. Then place in bowl with milk, egg, cardamom, sugar and salt. Mix well. Add flour and work into a dough, stiff enough to handle. Place dough on floured board and roll into a square. Place butter in middle of square and fold sides and ends over centre. Roll out and fold in this manner 6 times. Place in refrigerator until 2 hours before needed. Roll lightly, cut into strips and make into twists or figure "8" or any desired shape. Place on greased baking sheet and let rise in a warm room. Brush with melted butter and bake about 8 minutes at 400°F. Make a thin icing of beaten egg white and confectioner's sugar, and brush over the pastries while they are still hot.

Peasant Girl with a Veil　(Danish)

This is a delicious Danish pudding.

2 cups dried crumbs (your choice)
2 tbsp. sugar

1 cup tart jam
whipped cream

Crumble bits of graham crackers, rye bread, or other wafers to make fine crumbs. Add sugar and heat in slow oven until very dry. Cool and mix with any kind of jam. Mould and chill. Serve with whipped cream, garnish with extra jam.

Fruit Pudding (Finnish)

This favorite dish in Finland, was made with dried prunes in winter and served at breakfast for special guests. After Finns came to America, they used canned fruit to make it a special family treat.

4	cups bread crumbs	⅓	cup sugar
2	tbsp. butter	¼	tsp. salt
1½	cups milk	1½	cups drained preserves
2	eggs		(peaches, prunes or apples)

Place breadcrumbs in 1½-quart baking dish. Add butter to heated milk-just warm enough to melt butter. Lightly beat eggs, mix with milk and butter, add remaining ingredients, then pour over bread crumbs. Place baking dish inside a larger pan and add water in larger pan up to 1". Bake in 350°F oven 40-45 minutes, or until knife inserted 1" from edge of pudding comes out clean. Serve warm with cream. Yield: 6-8 servings.

Finsk Brod (Finnish "Bread") (Finnish)

2⅓	cups flour	1	egg, beaten
½	cup sugar	¼	cup coarse sugar
1	cup butter	⅓	cup finely chopped nuts

Blend flour and sugar, then cut in butter until fine crumbs. Working lightly with dough, shape until it holds in a ball. Divide dough in 6 pieces. On lightly floured board roll each piece into a 10" log, then flatten with knife to ½" thick. Brush with egg, sprinkle on coarse sugar and nuts. Cut in diagonal strips forming diamond shapes 1" wide. Place on greased cookie sheet. Bake in 325°F oven 10-12 minutes, or until edges are golden. Yield: about 4½ dozen cookies.

Tea Ring (Swedish)

1	yeast cake	1	cup milk, scalded
½	cup warm water	1	egg, beaten
2	tsp. sugar	2½	cups flour
2	tbsp. butter		butter, cinnamon, brown sugar,
¾	tsp. salt		raisins, nuts (optional)

Blend the yeast, water and sugar; let stand until liquefied. Add butter and salt to hot milk. Cool, add yeast mixture and egg. Stir in enough flour to make a soft dough. Knead on a lightly floured board until dough is elastic and does not stick to board. Set dough in greased bowl, cover, let rise to twice its bulk. Knead down, cover, and let rest 10 minutes. Roll into ½" thick rectangular sheet. Brush with soft butter, sprinkle cinnamon, brown sugar, raisins (or currants) and chopped nuts on dough, then roll like jelly roll. On a greased baking sheet, shape dough roll into ring. Cut every inch around ring with scissors, cutting almost through ring. Slightly turn each slice, brush ring with butter and cover. Let rise until double in size. Bake in 350°F oven 25-30 minutes. Remove from oven and, while warm, brush with light sugar icing and sprinkle with nuts if desired.

Joulutortut (Prune Pinwheels)   (Finland)

Pastry:

1 cup whipping cream	¼ tsp. salt
2 cups flour	1 cup soft butter
½ tsp. baking powder	

Filling:

2 cups dried prunes	½ cup sugar
3 cups water	1 tbsp. lemon juice

Glaze:

2 tbsp. milk	2 tbsp. sugar

To prepare pastry: In a large bowl, whip cream until stiff. Combine flour, baking powder and salt. Sift into cream, mixing well. With a wooden spoon, stir in butter until well blended. Press into a ball. Wrap dough in waxed paper and chill well, about 2 hours. To prepare filling: In a large saucepan, cook prunes in water until soft; drain. Pit prunes and put through food grinder or press through a sieve. Stir in sugar and lemon juice; mix well. set aside to cool. On lightly floured surface, roll out pastry to ¼" thickness and cut into 2½" diamond shapes. Cut a 1" slash from each corner towards centre. Place 1 heaping tsp. of cooled filling in centre of each square. Fold alternate points of slashed corners into centre to form a pinwheel or star. To glaze, brush pastries with milk and sprinkle with sugar. Arrange about 2" apart on ungreased baking sheets. Bake at 400°F about 10 minutes. Cool on rack. Makes 3-4 dozen.

Doughnuts   (Icelandic)

oil for deep-frying	1 tsp. vanilla
¾ cup sugar	2 cups flour
2 tbsp. butter	2 tsp. baking powder
2 eggs, beaten	½ tsp. salt
⅔ cup milk	½ tsp. nutmeg

Coating:

½ cup sugar	½ tsp. cinnamon

Heat oil to 375°F. Beat sugar and butter into beaten eggs. Add milk and vanilla. Sift dry ingredients and blend well with butter mixture. Use a teaspoon to drop dough into hot oil. Fry until dark golden brown. Drain.

Combine sugar and cinnamon. Roll well-drained doughnut balls into sugar mixture.

Vinarterta *(Christmas Cake)*   *(Iceland)*

This recipe was very popular on the Prairies. Icelanders shared it with friends and neighbours from many countries.

Cake:

1 cup butter	4 cups flour
1 cup granulated sugar	3 tsp. baking powder
3 eggs	½ tsp. salt
2 tsp. vanilla	¼ cup milk

Cream butter and sugar, beat in eggs and vanilla. Mix flour, baking powder and salt, then stir into butter mixture alternately with milk, forming a soft dough. Chill 20 minutes. Cut 8, 8" circles from waxed paper. Divide dough into 8 balls; press each ball to edge of each circle of waxed paper. Place circles into greased 8" round cake pans (if you have only 2 pans, bake 2 at a time). Bake in 350°F oven for 20 minutes, until light brown. Cool for a few minutes, then remove waxed paper.

Filling:

1½ lbs. prunes	¾ cup brown sugar
2½ cups boiling water	1 tsp. cinnamon
2 tbsp. lemon juice	1 tsp. cardamom seeds (optional)

Combine prunes and boiling water in saucepan; simmer about 20 minutes, until prunes are tender. Drain, saving liquid; remove pits; return prunes to liquid in saucepan. Add lemon juice, brown sugar, cinnamon and cardamom, if using. Cook until thick enough to spread. Mash until smooth. Cool. Spread each cooled cake with filling and stack layers with top layer bottom down. If cakes appear a little crisp, filling will soften them when stored. Store in tightly covered container several days before serving. If desired, spread thin butter icing on cake.

Van Meter and Erikson Families, Conjuring Creek area, ca. 1906

Krumkaka   (Norwegian)

This Norwegian specialty, traditionally made for Christmas, can be eaten plain or filled with whipped cream.

3 eggs
1 cup sugar
½ tsp. ground cardamom

1½ cups sifted flour
2 tbsp. cornstarch
½ cup butter

Beat eggs lightly. Add sugar, gradually beating until light in colour. Stir in cardamom. Sift together flour and cornstarch. Blend into cream mixture alternately with butter. Bake on a moderately hot krumkaka iron. Place 1 tbsp. of batter just off-centre on back half of iron. Bring top of iron down gently, then press firmly (don't squeeze out much batter). Scrape any excess batter from edges. Bake about ½ minute on each side, or until lightly browned. Remove from iron and quickly roll on cone-shaped form which comes with the iron. Makes 4 dozen.

Barenlie Crans (Cookies)   (Norwegian)

2 cups butter
2 cups sugar
3 raw egg yolks
1 tsp. vanilla
¼ tsp. salt

2 hard-boiled egg yolks, well mashed
4 cups flour (approx.)
1 egg white
sugar for dipping

Cream butter and sugar. Blend in raw egg yolks, vanilla and salt. Add mashed, boiled egg yolks and enough flour to make a soft dough. Roll dough into small balls. Lightly beat 1 egg white, dip top of each cookie ball into egg white, then into sugar, placing sugar side on cookie sheet. Bake in 350°F oven about 10 minutes.

Swenska Pepparkakor (Spice Cookies)   (Swedish)

4½ oz. butter
4½ oz. sugar
3½ oz. light syrup
½ oz. grated lemon rind
1 oz. almonds, blanched, chopped (optional)
½ oz. mixed peel, chopped

9 oz. flour
1 tsp. baking powder
2 tsp. ground cloves
1½ tsp. ground ginger
2 tsp. cinnamon
½ oz. flaked almonds (optional)

Heat butter, sugar and syrup in saucepan; do not boil. Remove from heat and cool slightly. Stir in lemon rind, chopped almonds and peel. Sift dry ingredients, add to mixture and knead well. Leave dough in cold place overnight until firm. On lightly floured board roll out dough thinly. Cut in 2" rounds, decorate with flaked almond, if using, place on greased cookie sheet. Bake in 375°F oven 8-10 minutes.

Riskrem (Norwegian)

This is a Norwegian Christmas Dessert. The finder of the almond gets a special gift.

¾ cup uncooked rice
4 cups milk
1 tsp. salt
½ cup sugar

½ cup slivered almonds
2 cups heavy cream
sugar
1 whole almond

In top of double boiler over boiling water, combine rice, milk and salt; cook, stirring often, until rice is tender, about 1½ hours. Stir in sugar and slivered almonds. Transfer to glass bowl; cover and chill 1-2 hours. Just before serving, whip cream, sweetening to taste and fold into rice mixture with the 1 whole almond. Yield: 8-10 servings.

Potato Torte (Norwegian)

½ cups sugar
4 eggs, lightly beaten
1 cup butter, creamed
¼ lb. nuts, chopped
5 oz. grated sweet chocolate
1 lemon, grated rind of

1 cup grated raw potatoes
2½ cups flour
2½ tsp. baking powder
1 tsp. cinnamon
½ tsp. cloves
½ cup milk

Add sugar and eggs to butter; beat until smooth. Add nuts, grated chocolate and lemon rind. Drain off excess water from potatoes; add potatoes to mixture. Sift flour with baking powder and spices. Add to potato mixture alternately with milk. Bake in springform pan in 325°F oven 1½-2 hours.

Christmas Dinner Dessert (Swedish)

4 eggs, separated
1 lb. dates, chopped
1 cup sugar
1 cup nuts
½ cup flour
1 tsp. baking powder

2 tsp. vanilla
¼ tsp. salt
4-5 cups fresh fruit
1 cup fruit juice
1 cup whipping cream
nuts (optional)

Lightly beat egg yolks and mix with rest of ingredients, except egg whites, fruit, juice and cream. Beat egg whites until fairly stiff, then fold into date mixture. Line a 12 x 16" pan with waxed paper. Spread dough in pan. Bake in 350°F oven for 30 minutes. Cool. Break half of cake in pieces on a platter. Over this slice fresh fruits. Break rest of cake over fruit, pat into shape. Pour fruit juice over top. Let stand 3-4 hours. Whip the cream and spread over dessert. Decorate with fresh fruit slices and nuts (optional).

WESTERN EUROPEAN

Mrs. L.C. Eckenfelder and children, Trochu, 1915

Western Europe

Belgium – Between 1899 and 1919, 1,016 Homesteads were taken by Belgians in the four western provinces. To the approximately 9,500 Belgians in Canada in 1910, another 7,000 were added before the outbreak of the first World War.

Netherlands – The Dutch, due mainly to the location and size of their country, have been world traders for centuries. Their contacts in many lands resulted in worldwide settlement. The majority of Dutch immigrants to Western Canada came via the United States, after the agricultural frontier was depleted there.

France – In 1878 the first French farm settlement in Alberta was founded at St. Albert, ten miles north of Edmonton.

The French were the first European inhabitants in Canada, dating back to the early 17th century. The first permanent settlement was in Quebec City in 1608. They made their way to the West as early as 1634. The first permanent settlement in Western Canada was established in 1818 when a number of French Canadians founded St. Boniface.

Swiss – The C.P.R. brought a number of Swiss Alpinists to the Rocky Mountains in 1912-13. The mountains were being opened up to climbing and the Swiss were to serve as guides.

Spain – Most of the emigration from Spain was to South and Central America, but there was a modest Spanish emigration of 2,000 to Canada in 1913 and 1914.

Italy – The first Italians came to work on the railroad during 1883-1914. In 1910 the CPR workforce totaled 8,576 of which 3,144 were from Italy. In 1900, 10,834 Italians were in Canada; from 1901 to 1910, 60,000 more emigrated to Canada.

Country-Style Hearth Bread (French)

1 pkg. yeast	3 cups flour
1 cup warm water	3 tbsp. cornmeal
¾ tsp. salt	½ cup water
1 tsp. sugar	1 tsp. cornstarch
1 tbsp. butter, melted, cooled	

In large bowl, blend yeast and warm water and let stand 5 minutes. Mix in salt, sugar, butter, 2 cups flour and beat vigourously for 5 minutes, until dough is very elastic. Stir in ½ cup more flour. On board, spread ½ cup flour, turn out dough and knead until very springy, about ½ hour. (The longer kneading time develops the desired texture). Add more flour if needed. Place dough in greased bowl, turning to grease all of dough. Cover, set in warm place and let rise until doubled in size. Punch dough down, then shape in smooth round loaf. Sprinkle cornmeal in a 6" circle on a large plate or board. Set dough on cornmeal, cover, set in warm place and let rise until doubled. Place an ungreased cookie sheet in 375°F oven as it is heating. With a very sharp flour-dusted blade, make 2 slashes on top of loaf about 1" deep. Gently slide dough onto hot cookie sheet and bake about 1 hour, until nicely browned. In a small pan, blend water with cornstarch and boil, stirring constantly. Brush cornstarch mixture over loaf after first 10 minutes of baking. Repeat 10 minutes later. Remove loaf from oven and cool on wire rack.

Suggestion: Serve with pâté, cheese or cold meat.

Savarin (French)

½ cup milk, scalded, then cooled until just warm	2 egg yolks
1 yeast cake	1 egg, beaten
¾ cup sugar	½ tsp. vanilla
4 tbsp. butter, melted	2 cups less 2 tbsp. flour
	fresh fruit (if desired)

Prepare milk. Add yeast to cooled milk; let stand 10 minutes. Beat sugar and melted butter, add egg yolks, beating until thick. Blend in beaten egg and vanilla. Add milk mixture alternately with flour. Cover, set aside in warm place, let rise 3 hours. Place dough in a greased tube pan. Bake in 350°F oven until it tests done. Remove from pan, fill centre with fresh fruit, sprinkle with sugar, if desired.

Brioche (French)

½ cup milk, scalded
½ cup butter
⅓ cup sugar
½ tsp. salt
½ cup lukewarm water
1 tsp. sugar

1 pkg. yeast
1 egg, separated
3 eggs, well beaten
3½ cups flour, sifted
1 tbsp. sugar

Cool milk to lukewarm. Cream butter well, then gradually add ⅓ cup sugar and the salt and cream together. Place lukewarm water, 1 tsp. sugar and yeast in bowl, let stand 10 minutes, then stir well. Blend in warm milk and butter mixture (disregard curdling, if any.) Beat yolk of separated egg, and mix with 3 beaten eggs and flour into warm mixture, then beat 10 minutes. Set aside in warm place, covered with a damp cloth, for about 2 hours, or until double in size. Beat batter well, cover with waxed paper and chill overnight. Next day, mix batter and place dough on lightly floured board. Cut off ¼ of dough and set aside. Cut remainder of dough into 18 pieces and form each into a ball. Grease muffin tins and place a dough ball in each well. Make a dent in centre of each dough ball. Cut smaller piece of dough into 18 pieces and make small balls. Lightly daub one side of small ball into cold water and press into dents of larger balls in muffin pans. Set aside in warm place, covered, for about 1 hour. Slightly beat remaining egg white with 1 tbsp. sugar and brush on top of each bun. Bake at 375°F for 15-20 minutes.

Mme. Corine Joly reading "La Survivance", in kitchen, St. Paul, 1929

Eenvoudige Bruine Boonensoep   *(Dutch)*
(Plain Brown Bean Soup)

10 oz. brown or black beans	¼ tsp. nutmeg (or more)
2 qts. cold water	5 tbsp. onion, chopped
¼ tsp. paprika (or more)	3 tbsp. butter
salt to taste	¼ cup flour
1 bayleaf	

Soak beans 12 hours in cold water; drain, then put in a saucepan with fresh cold water; add seasonings. Bring to boil, reduce heat and simmer 2 hours, or until beans are tender. Fry onions in butter until golden; add flour. Stir into soup and boil 15 minutes. Serve as is or rub through a sieve. Serve with strips of toasted bread.

Tomatensoep Met Gebakken Broodjes
(Cream of Tomato Soup with Fried Bread Cubes)

4 large tomatoes, quartered	2 tbsp. butter
1 onion, sliced	⅓ cup flour
2 bay leaves	parsley, finely chopped
salt	pepper
4 cups water	cream or milk

Place tomatoes, onion, bay leaves and salt in boiling water. Simmer 20 minutes and strain. In another pot, melt butter, add flour and mix in a little soup. When creamy, add a little more soup, until all is creamy and smooth. Add parsley, pepper to taste and milk. Serve hot – do not boil. Serve with fried bread cubes below.

Fried Bread Cubes: Remove crusts of 2 bread slices and cube. Fry in butter until golden. Serve separately.

Split Pea Soup   *(Dutch)*

1 lb. split green peas	1-1½ tsp. salt
1 medium carrot, diced	pepper
3 onions, diced	½ lb. metwurst sausage
3 potatoes, diced	or meaty ham bone
3 qts. cold water	

Place all ingredients in a soup kettle. Bring to a boil and boil gently 2 hours. Stir occasionally. If necessary, add a little more water. Serve hot.

Potage Verte (Green Soup)　(French)

1	bunch watercress leaves	2	slices bread
4	cups beef stock	2	tbsp. butter or shortening
1	potato, diced	1	hard-cooked egg yolk
	salt and pepper to taste		

Cook watercress in beef stock until almost done; add potatoes and cook until soft. Pour into sieve, saving liquid, press through sieve and add purée to stock in which it was cooked; keep hot. Brown bread slightly in 1 tbsp. butter, then cut into small cubes. Add minced egg yolk and remaining butter to soup, season to taste, add bread cubes and serve hot.

Potage Crème De Potiron (Pumpkin Soup)　(French)

1½	lbs. pumpkin	2	egg yolks
1	large tomato, halved	3	cups boiled milk
1	small onion, thinly sliced		salt and pepper
	butter	1	tsp. sugar

Peel pumpkin; cut in 3" lengths; place in pot with tomato, onion slices and a little butter. Do not add any liquids. Cover tightly. Cook in slow oven or over very low heat 1 hour. Remove from heat; rub through a sieve into another saucepan and stir in hot milk. Season with salt, pepper and sugar, and place over low heat. Mix egg yolks in a bowl, dilute with a little cold milk. Remove soup mixture from heat, add a little to egg mixture, stir, then add all egg mixture back into soup in pot. Stir and heat through, then serve with croûtons.

La Soupe Des Noces (The Nuptial Soup)　(French)

It is the custom in Perigord for the wedding guests to take this soup, in the middle of the night, to the newly married couple, barging into the nuptial suite with the hot soup, which the couple is forced to eat. By this time the guests, having wined and dined well, are very merry, and their intrusion is no doubt a noisy, disturbing-but-fun-affair!

6	large tomatoes, quartered		salt and pepper
1	onion, finely chopped	1	tbsp. vermicelli
	butter		toasted bread
1	qt. warm water		

Put tomatoes and onion in pot with a little butter and simmer about 15 minutes. Cover with warm water, bring to a boil, then simmer 1 hour. Season well with salt and pepper. Pour through sieve into another pot; rub tomatoes and onion through sieve as well. Bring to boil, then add vermicelli and a few pieces of toasted bread 10 minutes before serving.

Minestrone Soup with Ground Beef *(Italian)*

1 lb. ground beef
2 tbsp. oil
2 medium onions, thinly sliced
⅛ tsp. marjoram
1 garlic clove, crushed
1 bay leaf
2-3 cups red kidney beans

2 cups tomatoes
2 cups shredded cabbage
1 cup cooked rice
1 tsp. salt
¼ tsp. pepper
1 cup water

Sauté beef in oil until crumbled. Add onions, marjoram, garlic, bay leaf and sauté 5 minutes. Mash kidney beans in their own liquid and add with tomatoes to meat mixture. Over low heat continue to cook, covered, for 45 minutes. Ten minutes before serving add cabbage and rice and simmer 10 minutes. Season. Add a little water if too thick. Serve hot.

Bean Soup *(Italian)*

2 cups dry white beans
1 large onion, diced
1 large carrot, diced
2 celery stalks with leaves, diced
2 garlic cloves, crushed
½ cup chopped ham

¼ cup oil
salt and pepper to taste
seasonings of choice
½ cup chopped parsley
8-10 slices dried or toasted bread

Rinse beans then place in kettle. Cover with water; bring to boil; boil 3 minutes. Remove from heat, cover and set aside 1 hour. Drain, save liquid, put beans in a bowl, put liquid in soup kettle. In frying pan, sauté diced vegetables, garlic and ham in oil for 5 minutes. Add cold water to saved liquid to make 3 quarts; place on heat; add sautéed ingredients, beans and seasonings. Bring to a boil. Reduce heat and simmer, partially covered, 1½-2 hours, until beans are tender. Remove half of beans, purée and return to soup. Add parsley, stir and simmer 2 or 3 minutes. Before serving, put a piece of bread in each individual bowl. Ladle soup over bread. Garnish with grated cheese or parsley or pepper. Serve hot.

Gnocchi Al Brodo *(Butterball Soup)* *(Italian)*

1½ tbsp. butter
1 egg, separated
3 tbsp. flour
1 tbsp. grated Parmesan cheese
⅛ tsp. salt

white pepper
dash nutmeg
4½ cups clear beef broth
parsley

In a small bowl, cream butter and egg yolk thoroughly. Add flour, cheese and seasonings and mix well. Fold in beaten egg white to form a dough. Bring broth to a boil in a large saucepan, then reduce heat to medium and to a gentle boil. Drop dough by teaspoons into boiling broth; cover and simmer 10 minutes. Ladle into soup bowls. Garnish with chopped fresh parsley and serve hot.

Tortellini Al Brodo *(Tortellini Soup)*   *(Italian)*

1 whole stewing chicken	2 garlic cloves, minced
water and/or chicken broth to cover	2 tsp. salt
3 carrots, chopped	¼ tsp. white pepper
3 celery stalks, chopped	1 tsp. basil
1 medium onion, chopped	1 tsp. oregano
parsley sprigs	2-3 cups fresh tortellini (see below, or purchased)

Skin chicken, place in large pot, cover with water or broth and cook over medium heat, do not boil. As chicken cooks, a scum will come to the top – remove this with a spoon. When scum stops forming, add vegetables and spices. Cook about 2 hours, or until chicken is tender; remove it from pot. Cool and remove meat from bones, cutting meat into bite-sized pieces. Return meat to broth and reheat. When broth starts to boil, add tortellini and cook about 15 minutes.

Tortellini   *(Italian)*

Pasta Dough:

3 cups unsifted flour	2 tbsp. olive oil
2 eggs, lightly beaten	2 tsp. salt
2 egg whites	

To make pasta dough, put flour in a large bowl; make well in centre; add remaining ingredients. Mix until dough can be gathered into a rough ball. Moisten any remaining bits of flour with a few drops of water; press into the ball. Knead about 10 minutes, or until shiny and smooth, adding a little extra flour if needed. Let dough rest 10 minutes before rolling.

Filling:

2¼ cups cooked chicken, beef or pork, finely chopped	⅛ tsp. grated lemon peel
½ cup Parmesan cheese	⅛ tsp. nutmeg
2 egg yolks, lightly beaten	salt and pepper to taste
	6-8 qts. salted water

To prepare the filling, mix first 4 ingredients until thoroughly combined, then season. Take ¼ of dough (keeping rest moist by covering with a damp cloth), roll out dough until paper thin, cut into 2" rounds. Place ¼ tsp. chicken mixture in centre of each round. Moisten edges of each round, fold in half, pressing edges firmly together. Shape into little rings by stretching tips of each half circle slightly and wrapping ring around index finger. Gently press tips together. Best if cooked at once, but may be covered and refrigerated for a day or so. Bring water to a boil, drop in tortellini and stir gently with a wooden spoon to keep from sticking together. Boil for about 8 minutes, or until tender. Drain and serve with butter and Parmesan cheese. Makes about 80.

Note: Do not cook ahead if using in soup.

Les Balekes Ou Fricadelles *(Forcemeat Balls)* *(Belgian)*

2 lbs. pork, fresh ground
2 shallots or onions, chopped
   butter or lard
½ lb. bread soaked in milk
   salt and pepper
   nutmeg
6 tbsp. white wine
3 eggs, separated
   flour

pickling onions
soup stock, white wine or
   light beer
mixed herbs
garlic, chopped
few peeled potatoes
parsley

Place the pork in a bowl, add shallots or onions browned in the butter, then mix in bread soaked in milk. Season with salt, pepper, nutmeg. Add 6 tbsp. white wine, lightly beaten egg yolks and mix well. Add stiffly beaten egg whites and mix well. Make small balls, roll in flour, lightly brown in butter or lard along with a few pickling onions. Cover meatballs with stock, wine or beer, add herbs, garlic, salt and pepper and potatoes. Cover and simmer until potatoes are tender. To serve, transfer all to a hot dish and sprinkle with parsley.

Ragoût De Veau   *(Belgian)*

¼ cup butter
2 lb. breast of veal
6 medium onions, sliced
1 cup water
   salt and pepper to taste

¼ tsp. thyme
½ tsp. nutmeg
2 bay leaves
14 prunes
½ cup dry wine

Brown butter in a large pot or Dutch oven, and sear veal. Add onions, water, seasonings and bay leaves and cover. Cool slowly until meat is tender. Add prunes and wine, cook another 15 minutes, until the prunes are heated through.
Yield: 4-6 servings.

Quiche Bruxelle *(Belgian)*

½ lb. bacon, sliced
1 cup flour
½ tsp. salt
⅓ cup cold butter
3 tbsp. cold water

1½ cups sliced Brussel sprouts
½ lb. Swiss cheese, grated
2 eggs, beaten
1 cup heavy cream
   salt and pepper to taste

Cook bacon until crisp, drain and crumble. Sift flour with salt, cut in butter. Add water gradually, blending to form a pastry dough. Press pastry into a ball, then roll on a lightly floured board to ⅛" thick circle. Line 9" pie plate. Arrange Brussels sprouts, bacon and cheese in alternating layers on pastry. Combine eggs and cream with seasoning and pour over filling. Bake in 325°F oven 45 minutes, or until firm.

Jachtschotel *(Hunter's Stew)* *(Dutch)*

3 tbsp. butter
   as much cold meat as available, sliced
½ lb. cooking apples, peeled, sliced
3 medium onions, thinly sliced

12 large potatoes, boiled, sliced
   salt and pepper
1 cup stock

In butter, fry meat, apples and onions until golden. In casserole, alternate layers of sliced potatoes and meat mixture; add seasoning. Save enough potatoes for last layer but pour stock over ingredients before adding last potato layer. Then dot with butter. Bake in 350°F oven until cooked through and the top is browned.

Worsta Brootjis *(Pigs in Blankets)* *(Dutch)*

Filling:
½ lb. ground beef
½ lb. ground veal
1 egg, lightly beaten
½ cup milk

1 rusk, crumbled
½ tsp. allspice
   salt and pepper

Dough:
1½ cups flour
1 tsp. baking powder

½ tsp. salt
   milk

Combine the filling ingredients well. Mix together the remaining ingredients to make a soft dough. Roll into 4" long thin strips. Put a spoonful of meat mixture on each strip, roll dough tightly over filling and close ends. In a cake pan or on a cookie sheet bake in 350°F oven about 30 minutes. Makes 1 dozen.

Gebakken Witte Peen *(Fried Parsnips)* *(Dutch)*

2 lbs. parsnips
5 tbsp. flour
2 eggs, lightly beaten
⅔ cup bread crumbs or Dutch rusk crumbs

pinch salt
3 tbsp. butter
2 tbsp. melted honey

Cut the parsnips in pieces about ¾ x 3". Steam them until they are tender. Carefully make a paste by adding a small amount of water to the flour. Dip the parsnips into this paste and then roll them in the beaten egg. Roll parsnips in the crumbs, to which the salt has been added, and fry them in the butter and honey until they are golden brown. Yield: 6 servings.

Note: Parsnips need only a little imagination and they become exotic.

Wortels Met Boter En Peterselie Saus *(Dutch)*
(Carrots with Butter and Parsley Sauce)

10-12 large winter carrots
⅓ cup butter
3 tbsp. dark brown sugar

dash salt and pepper
½ cup finely chopped parsley

Steam carrots until they are tender. Melt butter with brown sugar and add salt and pepper. Add chopped parsley after all the brown sugar is melted in the butter. Stir, pour over the steamed carrots and serve. Yield: 6 servings.

Note: Parsley added to the carrots is a nutritional enhancement as it is high in potassium. Children love winter carrots cooked in this fashion.

Gestoofde Prel *(Creamed Leek)* *(Dutch)*

2 lbs. leeks, cut in 1½" pieces
2 tbsp. butter
2 tbsp. flour

vinegar
salt and pepper

Remove outer leaves and roots of leeks, wash, cut in chunks. In salted water simmer until tender-crisp. Drain liquid and save. In saucepan, melt butter, stir in flour; slowly add 1 cup of the liquid, bring to boil and stir often. Stir in vinegar, seasoning and leeks. Serve hot.

Sugar – One of the oldest flavorings, it has been used in Asia for several thousand years. The earliest form was liquid from sugarcane. Early Europeans used honey and fruit as sweeteners. Columbus took sugarcane to the West Indies, demand grew and sugar became a precious commodity. Sugarbeets were considered as an alternative in the 1800s. Available in cane and beets – raw, refined, brown, cubes.

Rode Kool (Spiced Red Cabbage)   (Dutch)

1   small red cabbage
1   cup water
¼   cup butter
3   cloves
2   apples, peeled, cored, sliced

2   onions, thinly sliced
1   tbsp. sugar
    vinegar (optional)
    salt

Cut cabbage in half, core, and shred thinly. In a saucepan, put the water and a little butter. Add cabbage, cloves, apples and onions; cover and simmer for ¾ hour. Add the rest of the butter, sugar and vinegar, and simmer 5 minutes. Serve hot.

A Dutch folk rhyme warns:

"Don't eat red cabbage on Monday, my friend;
A quarrel will throw you off the deep end.
Pots and pans will be hurled at your head,
And for days your poor face will be red."

Bieten Met Appelen (Beets with Apples)   (Dutch)

2   large or 4 small beets
5   tbsp. butter
1   onion, shredded

4   sour apples, peeled, chopped
1   tsp. salt
1½   tsp. nutmeg

Cook, peel and slice beets. Place in saucepan with rest of ingredients. Simmer until reduced to a pulp. Stir and serve hot.

Gestoofde Bieten (Stewed Beetroot)   (Dutch)

1½   lbs. beets, cooked
1   small onion, chopped
    salt
1   tsp. sugar

3   cloves
    dash of vinegar
    butter
2   tsp. cornstarch

Peel and slice beets after cooking. Place in pot with a little water, onion, salt, sugar, cloves, vinegar and butter and simmer, covered, 10 minutes. Make a paste of cornstarch and water; mix into beet mixture. Heat through and serve.

Koolsoorten Met Gehakt *(Dutch)*

(Cabbage and Meatballs Casserole)

1 cabbage, shredded
1 lb. ground beef or pork,
  (seasoned as for your own
  meatloaf, or see "Vleesballen")
butter

mashed potatoes
(see Aardappelpurée)

Boil cabbage until almost done, about ¾ hour. Drain. Make seasoned ground beef into balls. Brown in butter, then add a little water; cover and simmer until done. Prepare mashed potatoes (Aardappelpurée). In a casserole, place half of the cabbage, all the meatballs, then the remaining cabbage. Pour some of gravy from pan over, then cover with mashed potatoes. Dot with butter and brown in oven.

Vleesballen *(Meatballs)* *(Dutch)*

1   lb. ground beef
½   lb. ground pork
1   cup bread crumbs (or more)
½   cup milk
1   egg, lightly beaten
2   tbsp. grated onion

1   tsp. salt
    pepper
    seasonings of choice
2-3 tbsp. butter
2   cups beef stock

Combine all but the butter and beef stock. Blend well and shape into meatballs. Brown them in butter then pour beef stock over them. Cover and simmer 30 minutes.

Note: If gravy is desired, mix 2 tbsp. flour into the pan juices.

Aardappelpurée *(Mashed Potatoes)* *(Dutch)*

2   lbs. potatoes, peeled, boiled
1½ cups milk
¼   cup butter

nutmeg, grated
salt

While they are still warm, mash the potatoes until there are no lumps. Bring the rest of ingredients to a boil, then add mashed potatoes and stir well. With wooden spoon, whip mixture until white and creamy. Serve hot.

Variation: Put the potato mixture in a casserole, dot with butter and lightly brown the top in oven.

Moesgoed *(Barley and Raisin Stew)* (Dutch)

1 cup barley	¼-½ cup chopped mint leaves,
1 qt. buttermilk	2-3 slices bacon or cubed
1 lb. raisins	ham (optional)

Rinse barley, put in a kettle and cover with water. Bring to a rolling boil, then remove from heat and set aside, covered, 1 hour. Barley will expand. Stir in buttermilk and return to heat. Simmer about 1½ hours, stirring occasionally. Add raisins, mint and ham, if using. If bacon is used, fry crisp and crumble over Moesgoed. Serve hot or cold with syrup.

Gestoofd Konijn *(Stewed Rabbit)* (Dutch)

1 rabbit, cut up	celery, chopped
salt and pepper	bay leaf
butter	parsley
1 large onion, chopped	thyme
1-2 carrots, chopped	seasonings of choice

Rub rabbit pieces with salt and pepper and brown in butter. Add chopped vegetables and seasonings and a little water. Cover and simmer 1 hour, until half done.

Onion Sauce:

1 large onion, chopped	3 tbsp. flour
1 carrot, chopped	2 cups stock
celery chopped	1 tbsp. tomato purée
seasonings as for rabbit or of choice	salt and pepper
¼ cup butter	

To make the sauce, brown onion, celery, carrot and seasonings in butter. Remove vegetables from butter, then add flour to butter and brown slightly, stirring constantly. Add stock, tomato, salt and pepper and cook 10 minutes. Pour sauce over rabbit, cook 1 more hour, or until meat falls from bones.

Warme Ham-En Kaassandwiches (Dutch)
(Grilled Ham and Cheese Sandwiches)

8 thin slices stale bread	4 thin slices ham (not paper-thin)
4 slices Gouda or Edam cheese	drippings or butter

Remove bread crusts, cut all bread slices to the same size. Cut cheese and ham to fit bread, 1 of each between 2 slices of bread. Spread outside of bread with drippings and fry on both sides until golden brown and crisp.

Balkenbrij *(Scrapple)* *(Dutch)*

8 cups water
2 cups raisins
3 cups cracklings*
2 tbsp. salt

¼ tsp. pepper
6 cups buckwheat flour
shortening

Mix water, raisins, cracklings, salt and pepper in a large pan. Bring to a boil, then simmer 15 minutes. Stir in flour. Mixture will form a very stiff dough. Pat into a large cake pan. Chill. Slice thinly and fry in shortening until brown. Serve with corn syrup.

* Cracklings are the crisp residue left when pork is rendered.

Group at Paul de Beaudrup's ranch, Trochu, 1905

Chef's Meatloaf *(French)*

2 slices salt pork, thin 2" slices, diced
2 tbsp. onion, minced
2 lbs. ground beef
½ cup cooked tapioca

½ tsp. salt
¼ tsp. pepper
2 cups stewed tomatoes

Fry the salt pork, add onion and cook until golden brown. Add, including the drippings, to the remainder of the ingredients. Mix well; place in a loaf pan. Bake in 450°F oven 15 minutes, then reduce heat to 350°F and bake another 30 minutes. Serve hot or cold.

Béchamel Turnips   (French)

2 cups cooked, mashed turnips	½ tsp. salt
1 egg, lightly beaten	¼ tsp. pepper
2 tbsp. butter	béchamel sauce, below
¼ tsp. savory	grated cheese

Mix the mashed turnips with egg, butter and seasonings. Place in a buttered casserole. Top with Béchamel Sauce, below. Sprinkle with grated cheese. Bake in 400°F oven 25 minutes, or until the cheese melts.

Béchamel Sauce:

3 tbsp. butter	1 cup milk
3 tbsp. flour	

Melt butter in a pan, stir in flour until smooth. Gradually stir in milk and cook until smooth and thick.

Chou-Fleur À La Polanaise (Cauliflower) (French)

1 large cauliflower	½ cup butter
1 tbsp. vinegar	2 hard-boiled eggs
1 cup dry bread crumbs	

Wash cauliflower and separate into 6 portions. Crisp in salt water ½ hour, then plunge into boiling salt water to which vinegar has been added. This will keep the cauliflower white. Cook, uncovered, 20 minutes, or until tender; drain and set in a warm dish. Brown crumbs in butter, pour over hot cauliflower, garnish with sliced cooked eggs.

Suggestion: Try serving asparagus prepared the same way.

Olives – A fruit, olives were cultivated in Mediterranean regions since prehistoric times. They were mentioned in ancient Greek and Roman writings and Egyptian reliefs and artifacts.

Olive Oil – The oldest of cooking oils, it was used in ancient Athens. It was a symbol of the city's prosperity. Oil was used in cooking and in lamps. Olives were cultivated throughout the Roman Empire. It was believed that a daily dose of olive oil and wine was vital to longevity. The best quality is Italian, then Spanish, French and Greek.

Vis Ballen *(Fish Balls)*   *(Dutch)*

1½ cups boned, cooked fish
1 cup soft bread crumbs
2 tbsp. minced onion
¼ cup grated carrot
½ tsp. sugar

1 egg, beaten
salt and pepper
fish stock
2 tbsp. flour
½ cup minced parsley

Mix first 8 ingredients; roll into small balls. Heat fish stock to boiling, drop in fish balls, cook gently 45 minutes. Remove fish balls from stock onto platter. Mix flour with a little cold water, then add to stock to thicken. Stir in parsley, then pour over fish balls. Chill well. Serve cold.

Rissoles *(Filled Pastry Rolls)*   *(French)*

1 onion, chopped
2 cups chopped veal or chicken (white meat)
salt and pepper
1 egg, separated

1 cup water
1 tbsp. butter, melted
4 cups flour

Add onion to meat, season, add egg yolk and mix well. Mix together water, a little salt, egg white and butter. Pile up flour, make a well and slowly pour in liquid mixture. Work dough until smooth, then cut in slices and roll out into thin strips. Spoon chopped meat along strips, fold over, pressing edges together. Cut with small biscuit cutter, making small rissoles. Boil in lightly salted water 5 minutes, remove from water, drain. Bake in hot oven (400°F) 10 minutes until crust is golden on top. Serve hot.

Pâté De Foie Gras   *(French)*

2 lbs. veal liver
1 lb. fresh-ground pork
4 onions
4 small slices dry bread
4 eggs

¼ tsp. nutmeg
½ tsp. ground mixed spices
1½ tsp. salt
¼ tsp. pepper
raw pork fat, or salt pork

Grind liver, pork and onions one after the other, then dry bread, using fine blade. Separate eggs. Beat yolks, add seasonings, blend well with liver mixture. Fold in stiffly beaten egg whites. Coat sides of 1½-quart dish with raw pork fat. Pour in liver mixture. Set dish in pan of hot water. Bake at 300°F for 2 hours. Cool at room temperature. Chill 2 or 3 days. Serve cold.

Les Filets De Sole Au Cidre *(French)*

(Fillets of Sole with Cider)

A Frenchman might think he had grounds for divorce if all his wife served him was "just plain fish", whether steamed, fried or boiled, with no sauce or even melted butter.

	fillets of sole (as many as needed)	3-4	tbsp. butter
	salt and pepper		flour
2-3	onions or shallots, chopped	1	tsp. chopped parsley
1-2	cups cider, depending on number of fillets		

Place the fillets in an ovenproof dish, season with salt and pepper, sprinkle with onions, and pour cider over all. Bake in 350°F oven 15-20 minutes, until fish is tender. Drain cider into small pot, heat butter and stir in a little flour until mixture thickens slightly and is smooth. Add parsley, pour over fish and serve.

Poulet Aux Pêches *(Chicken with Peaches)* *(French)*

4	chicken breasts or chicken pieces	1	tbsp. parsley
4	tbsp. butter	4	or more preserved peaches, halved
2	small onions, finely sliced		
4	tbsp. brandy	1	cup chicken stock
2	tbsp. peach juice	1	tsp. cornstarch
½	tsp. salt	2	tbsp. heavy cream

Brown chicken in butter, add onions, cover and cook 15 minutes over low heat. Drain off most of the fat. Add brandy, peach juice, salt and parsley. On stove top, cover and simmer another 15 minutes. If necessary when doing a larger quantity, transfer to a casserole and bake in 325°F oven 15-20 minutes. Add peaches and cook 5 minutes. Skim off any fat remaining, then add stock, cornstarch and cream. Mix well, coating all the chicken, and heat thoroughly. Serve over rice.

Tapioca – Extracted from the roots of a poisonous plant, "cassava", tapioca was discovered ages ago by Indians of the Amazon who called it "manioca", "mani" Indian for "boy" and "oca" for "root". Legend is: Once, with great ceremony, a king buried his son. Later, according to custom, when the people dug up the boy's remains, no body was in the hole, just a large starch root. It is the main food for the poor in Brazil and other tropical areas. It is also a staple food for Pacific Islands natives.

Uses: in Brazil – in cakes, bread, soups;
    in North America – in soups, some main dishes and puddings.

Cheese Fondue (Swiss)

Switzerland gave the world Cheese Fondue. Traditionally, fondue should be stirred in only one direction.

"Golden Rule" for eating fondue: any guest who drops a piece of bread into the cheese sauce has to present a bottle of wine to the group or have the next fondue get-together. Ladies have to pay for their clumsiness by giving a kiss to each male guest.

Serve tea, white wine, or a small glass of kirsch (when served with Fondue, known as the "half-time drink") with Fondue.

1 garlic clove, halved	salt and pepper
8 oz. Swiss cheese, cut in strips	dash of nutmeg
1 tbsp. flour	2 tbsp. kirsch (or sherry)
1 cup dry white wine	crusty bread, cubed

Rub the inside of a ceramic pot, with the garlic clove halves. Blend cheese and flour in a separate bowl. Pour the wine into the fondue pot, heat over medium heat and stir, until bubbles rise to top (do not boil). Add cheese mixture slowly, ½ cup at a time, stirring constantly. Let each addition melt completely before adding another. Continue stirring until mixture bubbles slightly. Stir in seasonings and kirsch. Keep fondue bubbling while serving. Bread cubes should all have one crusty edge for dunking. Use long-handled fondue forks to dip bread in cheese, remove to plate, take off with a regular fork and eat with a regular fork – not the fondue fork. Use fondue fork only as a dipping fork. If fondue becomes too thick, stir in a little warmed wine. A "skin" will form at the bottom of the pot after the cheese is gone. Scrape out the skin and divide among all the guests – it's spicy and tasty.

Picnic lunch while ploughing (note oxen), Neutral Hills, 1910

Beignets *(Belgian)*

2 eggs, beaten
3 tbsp. sugar
1 cup milk
1 tsp. vanilla
1 cup flour

3 tsp. baking powder
1 tbsp. oil
1 apple, cored, peeled, thinly
   sliced
   icing sugar

To beaten eggs, add sugar, milk and vanilla. Mix well. Blend in flour, baking powder and oil, then stir in apples. Drop by spoonful into hot fat and fry to a golden brown. Remove, drain, cool and sprinkle with icing sugar.

Homemade Vanilla

1 vanilla bean, chopped
½ tsp. sugar

3 oz. vodka

Put in a jar, cover tightly, shake every day for a month, It is then ready to use.

Crème Caramel *(French)*

Caramel:
1¼ cups sugar

¾ cup water

Heat sugar in wide, flat pan over low heat, until brown. Slowly pour in water. Boil until sugar is dissolved and mixture turns golden brown.

Custard:
1 cup milk
1 cup cream
3 eggs, separated

½ cup sugar
1 tbsp. vanilla

Combine milk and cream, then scald. Beat egg whites until frothy, beat egg yolks and sugar and beat into egg whites until mixture is frothy. Add vanilla to milk mixture and, stirring constantly, gradually pour into egg mixture. Pour Caramel into ring mould or individual moulds, swishing caramel around in mould until it is well coated. Pour custard into mould, set in pan of hot water, and bake in moderate (350°F) oven 45 minutes, or until knife inserted comes out clean. Chill and unmould. Yield: 6 servings.

Jan In De Zak *(John in the Sack)*   *(Dutch)*

This steamed pudding got its name because it was made in a clean pillow case.

1 yeast cake	⅓ cup each raisins and
¼ cup lukewarm water	currants
3 cups flour, sifted	chopped peel (optional)
1 egg, lightly beaten	salt to taste
¾ cup milk, scalded and cooled to lukewarm	

Dissolve yeast in water. In a large bowl, add egg and milk to flour, stir with a wooden spoon until all the liquid is absorbed. Add washed and drained fruit and salt. Mix well. Add yeast mixture, blend well with a wooden spoon – dough will be sticky. Cover; let rise in a warm place 45 minutes. Sprinkle a clean wet cloth with flour. Roll dough into an oblong, tie loosely in a cloth, filling ⅔ full. Fasten ends firmly, stick safety pin in middle and steam 2-3 hours. Remove cloth. Serve hot with Molasses Sauce (see Ketelkoek met Stroopsaus below), melted butter and brown sugar. Do not cut with a knife, use a piece of string. Can be served cold with butter and sugar.

Ketelkoek Met Stroopsaus   *(Dutch)*
(Steamed Sultana Pudding with Molasses Sauce)

Pudding:

½ cup each raisins, currants	1 cup milk
butter	salt
bread crumbs	1 egg, beaten
2½ cups flour	

Rinse fruit and drain. Grease a pudding basin and lid. Coat with bread crumbs. Stir flour, milk, salt and fruit into beaten egg, and mix well. Pour into pudding basin (may be only ¾ full); cover tightly. Cook 2 hours in boiling water. When cooked, turn it onto a big plate and briefly dry under oven grill. Cut pudding in slices and pour Molasses Sauce over. Can be eaten hot or cold.

Molasses Sauce:

1 cup molasses	cinnamon
3 tbsp. butter	

Melt molasses and butter over low heat add cinnamon. Serve in gravy boat.

Haagse Bluf *(The Hague Bluff)*   *(Dutch)*

A favorite with Dutch children.

5 tbsp. red currant or raspberry juice	1 egg white
½ cup sugar	

Beat all together, 10 minutes or more. The longer one beats, the more one gets!

Oliebollen *(Oilballs or Deep-Fried Fruit Bread)*   *(Dutch)*

All Hollanders shout "oily" at New Year's when this very traditional dish is made and served.

1 tbsp. dry yeast	2 apples, peeled and chopped
2 cups lukewarm milk (½ cup more for high altitudes)	2 oz. peel
	oil to deep-fry
1 lb. flour	icing sugar
1 pinch salt	
8 oz. combined raisins and currants	

Soak yeast in ½ cup of the warm milk for 10 minutes; stir to dissolve. Put flour in bowl; make a hole in the middle for the risen yeast. Sprinkle salt away from yeast. Add warm milk in stages and stir until smooth. Add raisins, currants, chopped apple and peel. Let rise in a warm location, covered with a wet tea towel, for 1 hour. Then make into about 30 balls. Heat oil until almost smoking stage, and with 2 spoons pick up dough balls and drop in hot oil, 5 or 6 at a time. Cook until golden brown and crisp; place on paper towel. Sprinkle immediately with icing sugar and serve warm. They dry out very quickly, so cover them for later use.

To reheat – sprinkle some water over them, then heat, uncovered, for 10 minutes in 250°F oven. They become as crisp as when they were first fried.

Boterkaek *(Butter Cake)*   *(Dutch)*

1 cup butter, melted	1 tsp. baking powder
1 cup sugar	2 eggs, lightly beaten
1½ cups flour	sliced almonds (optional)
2 tsp. almond (or vanilla) extract	

Mix all ingredients in a bowl and stir vigorously until well blended. Spread batter in 9 x 13" pan or 10" springform pan. Sprinkle with sliced almonds. Bake in 350°F oven 30-35 minutes, until top is lightly browned.

Note: Batter will be heavy, and should have a moist cake-like texture when baked.

Sucre À La Crème   *(French)*

A bowl of this set out with a white cake makes a special treat. It is also wonderful over vanilla ice cream.

2 cups brown sugar	1 cup whipping cream

Combine sugar and whipping cream in a heavy saucepan. Bring to a boil and boil for 2 minutes. Remove from heat and cool. Stir occasionally. If it appears thin, beat it slightly as it's cooling. It should be the consistency of icing when cooled.

Hollandse Appelflappen *(Apple Fritters)*   *(Dutch)*

6 large apples, peeled, cored, sliced	1 tbsp. sugar
oil for deep-frying	1 egg, beaten
1 cup flour	½ cup milk
2 tsp. baking powder	powdered sugar
¼ tsp. salt	

Prepare apples. Heat oil. Combine dry ingredients. Add egg and milk and mix well for 3 minutes. Dip apple slices in batter, then deep-fry in hot oil until golden. Sprinkle with powdered sugar.

Variation: Add 1 cup currants or raisins to the batter.

Groningse Koek   *(Dutch)*

(Raisin Cake from Groningen province)

1 cup sugar	½ tsp. ginger
1 cup water	½ tsp. cloves
1 cup raisins	2 cups flour
½ cup butter	½ tsp. baking powder
¾ tsp. cinnamon	½ tsp. baking soda

In saucepan, combine sugar, water, raisins and butter; boil 2 minutes. Cool slightly; stir in the spices. Cool to room temperature, then fold in remaining dry ingredients. Grease and flour a loaf pan; bake in 325°F oven 1 hour.

Boterkoekjes *(Butter Cookies)*   *(Dutch)*

1¾ cups butter (at room temperature)	3 cups flour
1 cup sugar	

Mix butter and sugar until creamy. Add flour, mix well. Make into walnut-sized balls or smaller. Place on greased cookie sheet, flatten with glass dipped in milk. Bake in 300°F oven 15-20 minutes, until edges are just brown – do not brown whole cookie.

Old Dutch Sayings:

Every Dutch recipe starts with
> *"Pour a jigger of brandywine into the cook".*
> *"Not everyone is a cook who carries a long knife."*

Griesmeelpudding Met Bessensap *(Dutch)*
(Farina [Semolina] Pudding with Currant Sauce)

Farina Pudding:

4 cups milk	¼ cup sugar
vanilla	pinch salt
⅔ cup farina	1½ tbsp. butter
2 tbsp. cornstarch	1 egg, separated

Bring milk and vanilla to boil, add farina, cornstarch, sugar and salt, stirring constantly. Thickness of pudding can be changed by altering amount of farina. Reduce heat to low; carefully stir in butter and beaten egg yolk. Beat egg white stiff and fold into mixture. Mixture may be quite thick. Pour pudding into a mould rinsed with cold water. Chill.

Red Currant Sauce:

jar of red currant jelly	½ cup boiling water
2 lemons, juice of	

In saucepan, bring jelly, lemon and water to a boil, stir until smooth. Chill. Place pudding on a platter, pour sauce over and around it. Serve remaining sauce.

Poutines À Trou *("Puttins")* *(French)*

Pastry:

2 cups flour	½ cup brown sugar
3 tsp. baking powder	4 tsp. butter
½ tsp. salt	1 cup milk

Sift together first 4 ingredients. Add butter and mix well. Gradually stir in milk, mixing well. Roll thin, about ¼", and cut in round pieces, about 5" diameter.

Fruit Filling:

4 apples, diced	½ cup cranberries
½ cup raisins	

Mix fruits together. Place handful in centre of each round of dough, fold dough over fruit and shape into a ball. Place each "puttin" in cake pan. Make a hole ½"-¾" in centre of top of each ball. Bake in 325°F oven 20 minutes.

Molasses Sauce:

1 cup white sugar	½ cup molasses

Mix together sugar and molasses in a double boiler; bring to boiling point. As "puttins" are removed from oven, spoon at least 1 tsp. of sauce in hole.

Focaccia Alla Ceccobeppe *(Venetian Country Cake)* *(Italian)*

2½ cups stale very fine, bread crumbs	8 large eggs, separated
2 tbsp. butter	1 cup sugar
¼ cup raisins	1 lemon, grated peel of
⅓ cup candied fruit	pinch of salt

Sift bread crumbs and measure 2 cups. Put these in a bowl. Butter 3" high cake pan or ovenproof dish. Add remaining crumbs. Turn to coat pan. Discard excess crumbs. Cover raisins with cold water and let sit for 15 minutes. Drain and add raisins to fruit. Put 8 egg yolks and sugar in large bowl and beat until pale yellow and foamy. Add the reserved bread crumbs a little at a time. Stir in raisins and mixed fruit, then lemon peel. Add salt and stir carefully. Beat egg whites until stiff, then fold into bread crumb mixture very carefully. When mixed turn into prepared pan and bake at 350-°F for 45 minutes. Take out of oven, leave for 1 minute, then remove from tin. Sprinkle with confectioner}s sugar if desired. Leave on serving platter to cool. Serves 12.

Budino Di Patate *(Potato Pudding)* *(Italian)*

This dessert is surprisingly light.

¾ cup raisins	pinch salt
1 lb. potatoes, unpeeled	1 tbsp. flour
½ cup butter	⅓ cup sugar
½ cup light cream	3 eggs, separated

Cover raisins with cold water and set aside to plump up. Cover potatoes with cold water and boil until soft. Peel and mash them. Add butter, cream, salt and flour and mix together over low heat. Add the sugar, spices and egg yolks and mix thoroughly. Then pour mixture into a bowl. Beat egg whites until stiff, fold them into potato mixture. Pat the raisins dry and carefully stir into mixture. Butter and ovenproof dish, carefully pour mixture into dish. Bake in 350°F oven for 40 minutes. Serve hot with light cream. Serves 4-6.

Budino Di Avena *(Oat Pudding)* *(Italian)*

1⅓ cups oatmeal	4 egg yolks
2¼ cups milk	7 tbsp. sugar

Spread oatmeal on baking sheet and toast in 225°F oven for 20 minutes. Boil milk, sprinkle in the oatmeal, stirring constantly over low heat for 10 minutes. Press through sieve, adding a tbsp. or more of milk. Return to rinsed pan. Beat egg yolks until fluffy; add sugar and beat for another 5 minutes. Add to the pan. Cook gently for about 7 minutes stirring constantly until it is thickened. Dampen a mixing bowl with cold water and pour in mixture. Chill for 4 hours before turning out and serving. Serves 6-8.

Central Europeans

Most German immigrants did not come directly from Germany; but from German-speaking areas of Eastern Europe. Attracted by offers of land, local self government and linguistic freedom, German-speaking colonists had settled in Eastern Europe in the late 1770s and early 1800s. Growing nationalism in the late 19th Century, which brought pressures to assimilate and a scarcity of land, caused them to leave for North America. Of the Germans to come to the prairies before the first World War, 12% came from Germany, 44% came from Russia, 24% from other parts of Eastern Europe and 18% from the U.S.A. By 1900, people of German origin were the third largest ethnic group in Alberta, after those of British and native origins.

In 1889, 100 German-speaking families from Eastern Galicia in the Austro-Hungarian empire settled near Medicine Hat.

In 1894, German Moravians from Ukraine, seeking free land and religious freedom, established settlements named Bruderfeld and Bruderheim near Edmonton.

The Germans from Eastern Europe that had settled in Alberta were instrumental in encouraging their former Ukrainian neighbours in Galicia to also come to Alberta.

As all the settlements of German-speaking people were started along religious lines, much of their life centered around the church. In 1664, the first recorded German settler in Canada, Hans Bernard, purchased land near Quebec City.

Originally, few Canadians of German-speaking origin were from Germany. They came from Estonia in the north to the Black Sea in the south, from Alsace on the west to the Caspian Sea on the east.

In 1664, the first recorded German settler in Canada, Hans Bernard, purchased land near Quebec City. In 1885, Germans from Hungary became the first colonists to farm in Saskatchewan.

Mincemeat

Mincemeat goes back to the Middle Ages in Europe when crusaders brought back exotic spices from the East. These spices were used to preserve meat that was not cured by salting or smoking, as well as to flavor fruit. Various meats were chopped, mixed with chopped fruit and spices, placed in pottery containers, sealed with wax and stored for future use.

First recorded mincemeat recipe - 1486:

"a hare, 2 partridge, 2 pigeons, 2 covies strongly spiced and cooked" – "made craftily into the likeness of a bird's body, the meat stuffed into a pastry shell, and feathers placed over all."

Today, Mincemeat in Britain contains no meat while traditional American recipes do.

CENTRAL EUROPEAN

Jane Rummel, Basilici ranch, Kew, 1911

 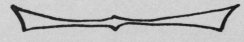

Schwartzesbrot (Black Bread)   (German)

1 pkg. yeast	1 tbsp. molasses
2 cups warm milk	½ tsp. caraway seeds, crushed
4-6 cups rye flour	1 tsp. salt

Soak yeast in a little of the milk. Mix about 2 cups rye flour with yeast mixture. Let rise a little. Add molasses, caraway seeds and salt, and enough flour so dough handles easily. Grease a bowl, add dough and grease top. Cover with clean towel and let rise in a warm place. Make into 2 loaves, place in loaf pans and let rise again. Brush with milk and bake in 350°F oven for 90 minutes.

Mohnbrotchen (Poppy Rolls)   (German)

1½ cups milk, scalded	4 cups flour
1 yeast cake	1 egg, beat egg yolk
½ tsp. salt	poppy seeds

Scald milk and cool to lukewarm. Dissolve yeast in milk, add salt. Stir in enough flour to make a fluid batter, like pancake batter. Cover and let rise several hours until double in bulk. This preliminary batter is called "rising". To the rising add the rest of the flour. Knead and beat dough thoroughly, until it is satiny and comes away from sides of bowl and off hands easily. Grease bowl, set dough in it, grease top of dough to keep it soft, cover, set in a warm place and let rise again to double in size. Shape into rolls, place on greased baking sheet and let rise again. Brush with egg yolk, sprinkle generously with poppy seeds. Bake in moderate oven (350°F) until nicely browned, about 20 minutes. Makes 12 large rolls.

Dumpfnudal *(Steamed Buns)*   *(N. German)*

3½ cups flour
1 cup warm milk
1 pkg. yeast
4 tbsp. sugar

1 tsp. salt
2 tbsp. soft butter
1 egg, lightly beaten

Dissolve yeast in 1/2 cup of the warm milk. Make a well in the flour, pour in the yeast mixture and the remainder of the milk. Sprinkle flour on top until it cracks, add sugar, salt, butter and egg. Knead until bubbles appear. Let rise for about 2 hours. Roll into 4 buns and let rise again. To cook, cover bottom of a frying pan with oil and sprinkle with salt. Cover. When grease sizzles, add ¾ cup warm water. Caution, this spatters so just lift lid enough to pour in water. Put in Dumpfnudal, turn heat down until sizzling stops, and cook about 12-15 minutes, or until water has cooked off.

Note: Do not peek while buns are cooking. When done, it will look like a dumpling and the steam should smell like yeast.

Pumpernickel   *(German)*

2 pkgs. yeast
1¼ cups warm water
1 cup rye flour
1 cup whole wheat flour
¼ cup dark molasses

2 tbsp. cocoa
1 tbsp. caraway seed
1½ tsp. salt
1½ cups + 2 tbsp. white flour
2 tbsp. cornmeal

Combine yeast and water in large bowl, let stand 5 minutes. Add rye and whole-wheat flours, molasses, cocoa, caraway seeds and salt. Stir in 1 cup white flour; scrape dough onto floured board. Knead, adding as little flour as possible, until dough is smooth and elastic, about 5 minutes. Cover and let rise until double in bulk, about 1 hour. Sprinkle cornmeal in centre of baking sheet; set aside. Punch down dough. On lightly floured board, knead dough and shape into ball. Place dough on cornmeal and press to form a 6" round. Let rise in warm place until nearly double, 30-40 minutes. Sprinkle additional flour on top of loaf, then bake in 350°F oven until loaf is a rich brown, about ½ hour, or until bottom sounds hollow when tapped. Serve at room temperature.

Racuchy *(Potato Pancakes)*   *(Polish)*

1¾ lbs. potatoes, peeled, grated
1 large onion, grated
1 egg yolk, lightly beaten
2 tbsp. flour
¾ tsp. salt

dash of pepper
2 tbsp. minced parsley
1 egg white, stiffly beaten
vegetable oil

With paper towels, press out as much liquid as possible from grated potatoes and onion. Place in a large bowl, add egg yolk, flour, salt, pepper and parsley; beat well. Fold in egg white. Pour ¼" oil in heavy skillet; heat until hot. Drop in 1 tbsp. of batter for each pancake, press with spatula, brown until crisp on both sides. Serve hot.

Weihnachts – Oder Sachsischer Stollen (German)
(Christmas Stollen)

8	cups flour, sifted	1½	cups raisins
1½	cups lukewarm milk	1½	cups almonds, grated
2	yeast cakes	½	cup candied lemon, chopped
1	tbsp. salt		or orange peel, chopped
1	cup sugar	2	tbsp. butter, melted
1	cup butter		

Prepare a firm yeast dough of flour, milk, yeast, salt, sugar and butter (see Stollen recipe method, below). Knead dough until it blisters. Knead in raisins, almonds and peel. Cover and let rise to twice its size. On lightly floured bread board, roll dough into an oval, about 1" thick. Fold in half, letting lower layer protrude. Pinch together firmly. Place on greased baking sheet and again let rise in a warm place. Brush with melted butter. Bake in hot oven (400°F) until done, 45-60 minutes. Brush with butter again while still hot. Sprinkle loaf with icing sugar or apply egg white icing.

Stollen (Christmas Tea Ring)   (German)

2	cups milk, scalded	2	tbsp. orange peel
1	pkg. yeast	4	eggs
6	cups flour	1	tsp. salt
½	cup butter	1	cup raisins
½	cup sugar	¼	cup candied fruit
1	tsp. grated lemon rind	¼	cup currants

Cool scalded milk to lukewarm. Add yeast and 3 cups flour. Let rise a little. Add rest of ingredients, including remaining 3 cups flour, and mix to make pliable dough. Knead dough and let rise. Divide dough in 2 parts, roll each into an oblong strip. Cut each part into two wide strips and braid. Let rise. Bake in 350°F oven for 20-25 minutes. Brush with glaze.

Glaze:

1	cup icing sugar	½	tsp. butter
2	tbsp. hot water		slivered almonds

Mix together first 3 ingredients and spread on hot bread. Sprinkle with almonds.

Coffee – Not known in Europe before the 17th century, coffee was used centuries earlier in Abyssinia and Arabia. It was grown in south-east Asia, then Jamaica, and South America. The first coffee house opened in England in 1652. Coffee was later introduced to North America. One legend about the discovery of coffee: About 300 A.D. a group of Christian priests fled to Abyssinia. One night a young priest, tending sheep, thought his flock "bewitched". Romping around the pasture, they had been eating leaves of wild coffee bushes. The elder priest tried the coffee berries, and couldn't sleep! A pleasant stimulant, coffee is picked ripe, then dried.

Gugelhupf (Almond Raisin Bread)   (Austrian)

½ cup sugar
½ tsp. salt
½ cup butter
½ cup milk, scalded
½ cup lukewarm water
1 pkg. yeast
1 tsp.sugar

2 eggs, well beaten
2½ cups flour, sifted
    fine bread crumbs
    whole almonds, blanched
½ cup raisins
½ tsp. grated lemon rind (or more)

Stir ½ cup sugar, salt and butter into scalded milk. Cool to lukewarm. In bowl, place lukewarm water, 1 tsp. sugar and yeast; let stand 10 minutes, then stir well. Stir in lukewarm milk mixture. Add eggs and flour and beat well for 5 minutes. Set aside in a warm place; cover with a damp cloth, and let rise until doubled in size, about 1½ hours. Sprinkle bread crumbs in well-greased 2-quart casserole, covering bottom and sides and shake out excess. On top of breadcrumbs put a layer of almonds. Stir batter well, and add raisins and lemon rind. Pour into casserole. Again let rise in a warm place for 1 hour, covered with a damp cloth. Bake in 350°F oven 40-45 minutes.

Bagels   (Jewish)

2 cups warm water
1 tbsp. sugar
2 tbsp. dry yeast
4 eggs, beaten

½ cup vegetable oil
1 tsp. salt
6-6½ cups flour

Poaching Liquid:
8 cups boiling water

¼ cup sugar

Glaze:
1 egg yolk
¼ cup milk

poppy or sesame seeds

In a large bowl, combine 1 cup of warm water with sugar. Sprinkle in yeast and let stand 10 minutes. Beat in remaining water, eggs, oil and salt. Beat in flour, a cupful at a time, working final cupfuls in by hand to make a soft sticky dough. Turn out dough onto a floured board; knead 5 minutes until smooth and elastic. Place dough in well-oiled bowl, turning to grease all over. Cover and let rise until doubled, about 1½ hours. Punch down dough and turn out onto floured board. Cut into 24-30 pieces. Roll each into 6" long cylinder, twisting and pinching ends together. Place on well-greased baking sheet. Cover and let rise for 20 minutes. Preheat oven to 450°F. To prepare poaching liquid, in a large saucepan, bring water and sugar to boil over medium-high heat. Add bagels 3-4 at a time, turning with chopsticks or wooden spoon handle, and cook 3 minutes. Remove with slotted spoon and place on greased baking sheet. To glaze, whisk together egg yolk and milk; brush over bagels. Sprinkle with poppy seeds or sesame seeds. Bake for 15-20 minutes at 450°F. Makes 2-2½ dozen.

German Bouillon

2 lbs. lean beef, finely chopped (no fat)
1½ qts. cold water
1 small onion, chopped
  bay leaf
  parsley
1 cup chopped outside pieces of celery root

2 egg whites, beaten with a little
  cold water
1 tbsp. lemon juice
1 tsp. salt
½ tsp. black pepper

Put meat in pot with next 5 ingredients. Cover and simmer 2 hours, then bring soup to a boil. Strain, return to pot and add rest of ingredients. Boil rapidly 5 minutes, strain through double cheesecloth, reheat quickly, if needed, and serve. Serve plain, or coloured slightly with lemon, wine or caramel.

Kattufel Suppen *(Potato Soup)* *(German)*

1 potato, sliced
1 onion, chopped
½ tsp. salt
1 tbsp. flour
1 tbsp. butter

1 cup milk
½ tsp. parsley
1 tsp. celery salt
⅛ tsp. pepper

Boil potato and onion with salt until soft. Drain and save 1 cup of liquid. Mash potato and onion. In a saucepan, blend flour and butter, then add milk and potato liquid. Add mashed potato mixture, parsley, celery salt and seasoning. Stir constantly for a few minutes and serve hot. Serves 2

Ham and Bean Soup *(German)*

1½-2 lbs. smoked ham and bone
1 medium onion, halved
1½ qts. cold water
1½ cups diced potatoes
2-3 cups freshly cut green
  or yellow beans

½ tsp. parsley
1 tsp. savory or dill
½ cup heavy cream
  or sour cream (optional)

Cook smoked ham and onion in the water in a 4-quart pot for 2 hours. Remove ham and onion; strain broth. Add potatoes, beans and herbs to broth and boil until potatoes are tender, but not overcooked. Remove meat from bone; cut finely and return to soup. Before serving, stir in cream OR reserve cream to be added to individual bowls, as desired. Yield: 6-7 servings.

Kartoffelsuppe *(Potato/Sauerkraut Soup)* *(German)*

1 qt. sauerkraut, drained	½ lb. salt pork, diced
1 qt. diced potatoes	1 cup flour

Cover drained sauerkraut with cold water. Add potatoes and cook until soft. Fry salt pork until light brown, add to potatoes and sauerkraut. Save fat in pan. Stirring constantly, mix flour into fat until well browned, add to soup and stir until flour is dissolved. Serve hot.

Brot Suppe *(Bread Soup)* *(German)*

few slices stale, dried bread, preferably crusts
3 cups veal or beef stock
salt and pepper
1 egg yolk, beaten

2-3 eggs, hard-boiled
cooked sausages or smoked meat
parsley, fried

Break bread in small pieces, put in a pot and pour in lukewarm stock. Let stand 10 minutes, until bread is thoroughly soaked. Heat and stir until mixture comes to a boil. Add seasoning, and simmer ½ hour. Soup should be smooth. Any lumps of bread should be crushed and stirred well. Reheat – do not boil. 5 minutes before serving, stir 1-2 tbsp. of hot stock into beaten egg yolk, and add back to soup. 2-3 minutes before serving, stir in sliced hard-boiled eggs and sausages or meat. Sprinkle with fried parsley and serve.

Meat Market and Post Office, Seven Persons, 1911

Potato Soup (German)

10-12 medium potatoes
2 medium onions
water
1-2 tsp. savory
½ tsp. salt
1 cup heavy cream
2½ cups buttermilk
3-4 tbsp. flour in a little water
salt and pepper to taste

Peel, wash and cube potatoes. Chop onions. Place in a pot of water. Add savory and salt to taste. Boil until potatoes are tender. Do not drain. Remove from heat, cool a few minutes. Add cream and buttermilk. Return to medium heat, thicken with water and flour mixture. Season with salt and pepper. Serve hot.

Chicken Soup (Mennonite)

1 chicken, cut in pieces
water
2 onions, sliced
salt and pepper
3 heads dill or 1½ tbsp. dill seed in a small cheesecloth bag
4-5 potatoes, chunked
6-7 carrots, chunked
½ cabbage, coarsely shredded

In a large pot, place chicken, enough water to thoroughly cover chicken, onions, and seasonings. Cook until chicken is tender. Bone chicken and return meat to pot. Add potatoes, carrots and cabbage. Depending on how "dilly" you want the soup, add water accordingly. Simmer at least 1 hour. Serve hot with buns and lots of butter.

Barszcz (Soup) (Polish)

1 cup rolled oats
3 qts. water
1 lb. spareribs
1 medium onion, sliced
2 cups cooked, diced beets
2 eggs, beaten
2 tbsp. flour
sour cream to garnish

Simmer oats in water 1 hour. Drain, save liquid. In pot, cover ribs and onion with fresh water; simmer until the meat is done and comes off the bones. Remove bones. Drain, adding liquid from ribs to oatmeal liquid. Cut meat in cubes. Add oatmeal, meat and beets back to liquid. Bring just to a boil. Add eggs to flour, mix well, and blend into soup to thicken. Serve hot, with sour cream if desired.

Weiner Schnitzel *(Vienna Schnitzel)* *(Austrian)*

This is a very simple and plain method.

very thin veal slices	fine bread crumbs
salt and pepper	butter
1-2 egg yolks, beaten	lemon slices (optional)
flour	

If the veal is not cut very thinly, pound it a little. Add seasoning to beaten egg yolks. Dip veal slices in flour, then in egg yolks, then in breadcrumbs. As veal slices are thin, cook only a few minutes in hot butter, until golden on both sides. Serve immediately on a hot dish. Garnish with lemon slices if desired.

Erdapfel-Nudeln *(Potato Quenelles)* *(Austrian)*

3-4	large potatoes, boiled	2	tbsp. grated Parmesan cheese
	flour		salt and pepper
1-2	eggs		bread crumbs

Boil potatoes in salted water; mash while hot. Cool, place on a board, mix to a stiff paste with flour, egg, cheese and seasonings. Roll into a sausage-like roll(s) about 1" thick. Cut into 1" lengths and dry about 1 hour. Boil in salted water or stock 10 minutes, or until they rise to top. Drain, fry lightly, sprinkle with bread crumbs and Parmesan. Can be served with a tomato sauce.

Zweibelkuchen *(Onion Pie)* *(German)*

4	slices bacon	1	tbsp. flour
2	cups peeled and chopped onions	½	tsp. salt
2	eggs, well beaten	¼	tsp. pepper
1	cup sour cream	1	unbaked pie shell

Preheat oven to 400°F. Sauté bacon until crisp; drain most of the fat from the pan. Add onions and sauté until they are clear. Set aside to cool. Beat eggs and sour cream together. Sprinkle flour over top and beat in. Add salt and pepper. Prick bottom of pie shell with fork. Spread onions and bacon over the dough. Pour the sour cream mixture over the top. Bake for 15 minutes. Reduce heat to 350°F and bake for another 15 minutes, until pie is browned. Serve hot.

Birocks (Cabbage Buns)   (German)

Dough:

1 cup milk	2 tbsp. sugar
1 cup boiling water	1½ tsp. salt
2 tbsp. shortening	6 cups flour
1 pkg. yeast	

Scald milk, add to boiling water and the shortening in a large bowl. Cool to luke-warm. Add yeast. Stir until dissolved, add sugar, salt and 3 cups of flour. Beat until smooth; add remaining flour and knead until smooth. Rub a clean bowl lightly with shortening. Rub ball of dough on sides of bowl to coat all surfaces. Cover and let rise until double in bulk.

Filling:

1-2 lbs. lean ground beef	1 large or 2 small cabbages, shredded
2 large onions, diced	salt and pepper to taste

Brown beef with the onion. Add shredded cabbage, salt and pepper. Cook over low heat until cabbage is limp. Roll the dough until thin. Cut into 4" squares. Place a generous amount of filling on each square. Join opposite corners of dough and press edges until well sealed. Place sealed-side down on a cookie sheet and bake at 400°F until nicely browned. Brush with butter when removed from oven.

Sauerbraten   (German)

3 lb. beef roast	1 tsp. salt
½ bottle red wine	1 tbsp. sugar
½ cup vinegar	4 tbsp. flour
1 cup water	salt
1 large onion	pepper
1 carrot	butter
1 bay leaf	flour or cornstarch, in water
2 cloves	½ cup whipping cream or sour cream

Start to marinate meat 2-3 days before you wish to serve it. Place wine, vinegar, water, onion, carrot, bay leaf, cloves, 1 tsp. salt and sugar in a saucepan and bring to a boil. Cool. Place meat in a nonmetal container and pour marinade over it. Refrigerate for 2-3 days, turning twice daily. Drain the meat and wipe dry; reserve the marinade. Mix flour, salt and pepper and rub into meat. Heat butter in a Dutch oven and brown meat on all sides. Strain the marinade, add ¾ cup to the meat. Cover and simmer for 3 hours. Add more marinade if necessary. Remove meat from the pot and make gravy with the drippings. To make gravy, thicken the drippings with a little flour or cornstarch blended first in cold water. Just before serving add a little whipping cream or sour cream. If you use sour cream, put some in a cup and add some of the hot mixture to it. Add this to the gravy in the pot and heat but do not boil or the gravy will curdle.

Rinderrouladen (German)

4 oz. bacon, diced
4 oz. onion, diced
1 round steak, ⅛" thick, cut into
   4 pieces, or 4 thin slices sirloin steak

mustard
salt and pepper
3 oz. fat
1-2 tsp. flour

Cook bacon slightly, set aside. Cook onion until barely translucent, set aside. Spread steak with mustard, salt and pepper. Add bacon and onion. Roll like jelly roll. Secure with skewers and/or string. Brown well on all sides in heated fat. Add 1 cup water. Cover and cook slowly 2-2½ hours on top of stove or in 325°F oven, turning often, adding water if necessary. Remove from pan, place on serving platter and keep warm. Stir flour and water into meat juices and make gravy. Season to taste. Pour over rouladen and serve hot. Yield: 4 servings.

Suggestion: Paprika, lemon, tomato paste or heavy cream may be added to gravy.

Huhn Mit Reis (Chicken with Rice) (German)

1 frying chicken
  flour (approx. 3/4 cup)
½ tsp. salt
⅛ tsp. pepper
  oil

1½ cups uncooked rice
1 tsp. salt
¼ tsp. pepper
3 cups boiling water
2 tbsp. butter

Cut chicken into large pieces. Shake and coat pieces in flour seasoned with salt and pepper. Fry in hot oil until brown. Place browned chicken pieces in a large casserole. Add rice, 1 tsp. salt and ¼ tsp. pepper; cover with boiling water and dot with butter. Cover and bake in 350°F oven for 1½ hours. Yield: 4-6 servings.

Ginger Meatballs (German)

1 lb. lean ground beef
1 egg, beaten
¾ cup soft breadcrumbs
1¾ cups water or beef broth
¼ cup chopped onions
½ tsp. salt

dash pepper
seasonings of choice
⅓ cup packed brown sugar
¼ cup raisins
2½ tsp. lemon juice
½ cup coarsely ground gingersnaps

Combine beef, egg, breadcrumbs, ¼ cup of the water or broth, onion, salt and pepper. Shape into balls, about 1½" diameter and set aside. In large skillet bring remaining water or broth to boil, add seasonings of choice, sugar, raisins, lemon juice and gingersnaps. Stir until combined. Add meatballs to mixture and simmer, uncovered, 20 minutes, or until meat is no longer pink, stirring occasionally. Serve with noodles or mashed potatoes.

Karfen Polnisch *(Christmas Carp)* *(German)*

½ cup dried cherries	1 bay leaf
2½ lbs. carp	salt and pepper
butter	1 cup water
1 celery stalk, finely chopped	1 bottle dark beer
1 onion, finely chopped	2" sq. of gingerbread, grated
1 yellow turnip, finely chopped	grated peel of half a lemon
1 parsley root, finely chopped	½ cup chopped almonds
2 cloves	¼ cup raisins
peppercorns	sugar

Soak cherries for an hour. Pit and stew until tender. Clean fish and cut in desired-size pieces. Melt butter, add chopped vegetables and cook over low heat. Add spices, cherries and seasonings. Combine water and beer and pour over mixture. Place fish in mixture and simmer until done. Add gingerbread, peel, almonds and raisins. Add sugar to taste. Bring to boil and serve immediately. Yield: 4 servings.

Variation: Substitute gingersnaps for gingerbread.

Suggestion: Serve with potato dumplings and sauerkraut.

Rollmopse *(Collared Herring)* *(German)*

Extensive use is made of herring in Germany, both fresh and salted.

fresh herring	wine vinegar
gherkins, thinly sliced	mustard seed
capers	lemon slices, thinly sliced
shallots, sliced	peppercorns
mustard	onions, thinly sliced
herring roe	olive oil

Remove head and bones from herring; divide into fillets. On each fillet put a layer of gherkins, capers, shallots and mustard. Roll up each fillet and secure with skewers. Put in jar with herring roe, cover with vinegar, mustard seed, lemon, peppercorns and onion. Cover the jar, let stand a few days in cool place. When ready to serve, add a little olive oil.

Pickled Cabbage *(Mild Sauerkraut)*   *(German)*

yellow or fall cabbage   salt
– NEVER juicy green cabbage   water

Knife-cut cabbage, medium coarsely (not finely). Pack firmly in warm quart jars (do not pound in until juice shows). Add 1 tsp. salt to each quart; fill jar with boiling water and seal tightly. Place in a warm place. You can use this in 2-3 weeks; it will keep forever.

Pickled Cabbage Dinner   *(German)*

spareribs, or pork roast or cooked   potatoes
  pork hocks or wieners   2 quarts drained mild sauerkraut

Place meat in roaster. Put peeled potatoes, cut in half, on the pork. Cover with drained mild sauerkraut, reserving the drained salt brine. Add ½ cup of the sauerkraut brine and ½ cup of water. Roast at 300°F for a couple of hours; add water if it gets dry.

Sauerkraut Salad   *(German)*

A husband from Scotland said, "Sure it will keep forever, no one will eat it." I asked him to just taste it and he did, and reluctantly said – "It is really good!"

1 qt. sauerkraut   3 celery stalks, diced
1 cup sugar   ¼ cup vinegar
1 medium onion, diced

Mix together, put in jars and refrigerate. Keeps indefinitely.

Essec Fleish *(Sweet and Sour Beef)*   *(Jewish)*

2 onions, sliced   2-3 gingersnaps, crushed
2½ lbs. beef chuck   2 lemons, juice of
  water   ¼ cup brown sugar
2 tbsp. flour   ¼ cup white sugar
  fat   salt and pepper

Place onions, meat and water in pot, cover and simmer 1 hour. Brown flour in frying pan; add enough hot water to form a thin gravy. Add gingersnaps to gravy and simmer 20 minutes. Add gravy and remaining ingredients to meat. Bake in 250°F oven 2 hours.

Hirshonsaltz Keachla (Ammonia Cookies) (German)

Made mostly during the Christmas Season.

2 tbsp. baking ammonia*
1 cup milk (can be sour)
6 eggs
3 cups sugar

1 cup soft butter
3 cups flour
1 tsp. lemon flavouring
1 cup sour or sweet cream

Dissolve ammonia in a little of the milk. Mix all ingredients into a soft dough and let dough set in cool place overnight. Roll out dough to ½" thick. Cut with cookie cutters. Bake in 375°F oven until light brown. (Watch carefully so they don't burn.) Ice, while warm, with powdered frosting and sprinkle with coconut or coloured sugar.

*Baking ammonia can be purchased at most bakeries.

Nusskipfel Dough (Nut Crescents)   (German)

Dough:

1 yeast cake
1 scant cup milk
4½ cups flour
2 eggs

1 tsp. salt
7 tbsp. butter
5 tbsp. sugar
3 tbsp. melted butter

Dissolve yeast cake in warmed milk. Add other ingredients, except 3 tbsp. melted butter. Knead well. Let dough rise. Roll out ½" thick. Cut into triangles. Brush melted butter on triangles.

Hazelnut Filling:

1½ cups chopped hazelnuts
5 tbsp. sugar

2 tbsp. water

Mix filling ingredients. Spread filling on each triangle, roll up tightly and shape into crescents. Place on greased baking sheet. Let rise again. Bake in hot oven (400°F) until nicely browned, 15-20 minutes. While still warm, spread with your favourite vanilla icing. Yield: 1½ dozen.

Portzelky (New Year's Eve Cookies)   (Mennonite)

1 tsp. sugar	¼ cup sugar
1 cup warm water	2 tsp. salt
1 pkg. yeast	1-1½ cups raisins, washed
1 cup milk	1 tsp. baking powder
¼ cup cream	2 eggs, beaten
¼ cup butter, melted	3½ cups flour

Dissolve sugar in warm water. Sprinkle yeast over and let stand 10 minutes. Combine milk and cream and scald. Stir in melted butter, sugar and salt and cool to lukewarm. Add raisins and baking powder and stir to blend. Add beaten eggs and yeast. Stir to blend and add flour. Mix until well blended. The dough must be soft to have a tender cookie. Cover and let rise until double in bulk – 1-1½ hours. Heat oil to 375°F. Do not stir the dough. Spoon it out from the edges rather than from the centre. Drop dough by small tablespoons into hot oil. Cook approximately 1½ minutes on each side. Drain on absorbent paper and shake in icing sugar.

Pfeffernusse (Peppernuts)   (German)

1 large egg	½ tsp. each cinnamon and allspice
¾ cup fine sugar	¼ tsp. each ground cloves and
¼ cup honey	cardamom
2 tsp. ground almonds	⅛ tsp. black pepper
½ tsp. grated lemon rind	rum and icing sugar if desired
2 cups flour	
½ tsp. baking powder	

In a large bowl, beat egg, sugar and honey until light and fluffy. Stir in almonds and lemon rind. Sift together flour, baking powder, cinnamon, allspice, cloves, cardamom and pepper. Work into sugar mixture until a smooth rather firm dough forms. Chill dough at least 2 hours. Form dough in long rolls 1" in diameter. Cut into ½" slices and roll each slice in a small ball. Place on greased baking sheets and allow to dry for 2-3 hours. Bake in 300°F oven until cookies are light brown in colour and firm to touch, about 15 minutes. Remove from oven, let cool slightly and sprinkle with rum and icing sugar if desired. Store in an airtight container. Makes 6 dozen cookies.

Nuts – Nuts have been used as a source of food and oil for centuries. Early Romans served sugar-coated almonds for special occasions. When the Spaniards came to America, the Aztecs were already using peanuts and pecans. Almonds, pistachios, walnuts are used extensively in the Middle East. Peanuts and cashews are used in Indonesia and the Far East; peanuts, hazelnut and almonds are used in many parts of Africa.

Windbeutel (Cream Puffs)   (German)

1 cup water	1 cup flour
½ cup butter	4 eggs
1 tbsp. sugar	1 cup, or more, whipped cream
⅛ tsp. salt	

Combine water, butter, sugar and salt over low heat. When boiling point is reached, add flour all at once. Stir to form a firm dough. Remove from heat and, one by one, beat in eggs and stir to a smooth batter. Scoop batter by tablespoons onto a greased baking sheet, forming tight, somewhat high mounds 2" apart. Bake in 425°F oven 15 minutes. Reduce heat to 350°F and bake 15-20 minutes longer. Be sure they are thoroughly baked or they will collapse. Cool, cut a slit in 1 side, and fill with whipped cream.

Deutschekuchen (German Kuchen)   (German)

Dough:

½ cup shortening	1 tsp. lemon flavoring
⅓ cup sugar	1 pkg. yeast dissolved in
2 cups milk, scalded	½ cup lukewarm water
3 eggs, well beaten	5-5½ cups flour
1 tbsp. salt	enough thinly sliced fruit for 6 pies (apples, peaches, blueberries)

Add shortening and sugar to scalded milk. Cool. Add remaining ingredients (except fruit) in order given. Let rise. Knead down. Let rise a second time. Roll out thin with a rolling pin. Place dough in 6, 9" pie plates; divide fruit into pans.

Custard:

1 egg	¼ cup sugar
¾ cup farm cream (or evaporated milk)	1 tsp. vanilla

Blend custard ingredients well. Spoon over fruit.

Crumbs:

½ cup melted butter	2 cups flour
½ tsp. vanilla	1 cup icing sugar

Combine all ingredients and mix until texture is like crumbs. Cover custard with crumbs. Bake in 375°F oven about 20 minutes, until crumb crust is brown.

Guglhupt *(Pan Dumplings)* *(Austrian)*

2 tbsp. yeast
1 cup milk
3½-4 cups flour
¼ lb. butter, melted (½ cup)

3 tbsp. sugar
2 tsp. lemon rind
2 eggs, slightly beaten

Sprinkle yeast over lukewarm milk; let soften. Mix all together into a soft dough, set aside and let rise.

Nut Filling:

¾ cup of any of poppyseed, almonds, other nuts, ground
1-2 tbsp. sugar
½ cup raisins

¼ cup milk
lemon rind, cinnamon and rum to taste

Cream Cheese Filling:

½ lb. cream cheese
1-2 tbsp. sugar
½ cup raisins

cinnamon
1 egg yolk

Plum Jam Filling:

1 cup jam or cooked prunes, mashed

rum
cinnamon

For each filling, combine all ingredients in a small bowl. When the dough has risen, take pieces of it, about the size of a walnut. Flatten in the palm of your hand, put in one of the fillings and put balls in a greased tube pan. Use up all the dough and as much of the fillings as possible. Mix up the dumplings as they are placed in the pan. Cover and let rise until double in size. Bake in 375-400°F oven for 45 minutes, or until brown.

Carrying Christmas Tree home, Kew, 1926

Lebkuchen *(Christmas Cakes)* (German)

1 cup shortening	1 qt. molasses
2 cups sugar	2 cups black coffee
2 tsp. baking soda	1 oz. anise seed
salt	½ lb. citron, chopped
flour to make stiff dough	½ lb. nuts, chopped

Cream shortening and sugar. Sift baking soda and salt with some flour. Blend liquids, alternate with flour until well mixed. While dough is soft, add anise seed, citron and nuts. When dough is stiff, cool in refrigerator. On a lightly floured board, roll a little at a time. Cut with oval cutter. Place on cookie sheet. Bake in moderate (350°F) oven until brown. When cookies cool, spread with a little frosting. Makes lots and will keep a long time.

Frosting:

¼ cup milk   powdered sugar

Combine to make a thin frosting.

Kolachies (German)

Sweet Dough:

1 cup milk	½ cup lukewarm water
½ cup sugar	1 tsp. sugar
¼ cup butter	2 eggs
1 tsp. salt	4½-5½ cups flour
2 tbsp. or 2 pkgs. yeast (not instant)	

To make dough, scald milk. Add sugar, butter and salt. Let cool. Dissolve yeast in water and 1 tsp. sugar. In bowl, beat eggs and add milk mixture and yeast. Add 1½ cups flour. Add more flour, 3-4 more cups, to make soft dough. Let rise covered, ½ hour and use.

Plum Filling:

dry bread crumbs	cinnamon
prune plums	½ cup sugar

Sprinkle dough with dry bread crumbs, enough just to cover. Split and pit prune plums; arrange cut side up over entire dough; sprinkle with cinnamon and sugar.

Topping:

½ cup flour	⅓ cup butter
½ cup brown sugar	

To make the topping; combine flour and brown sugar. Cut in the butter, cover the dough and filling. Bake at 350°F about 30 minutes. Serve warm.

Note: This dough also makes good buns. After forming buns, let rise until double, about 1 hour. Bake 20 minutes at 350°F.

Apfeltaschen (Apple Pockets)   (German)

2 cups flour	1 tsp. vanilla
1 tbsp. sugar	3-4 apples, peeled and grated
1 cup butter	apricot jam
1 cup cottage cheese	icing sugar, milk, vanilla

Combine flour and sugar. With pastry blender, cut in butter. Add cottage cheese and vanilla; mix thoroughly, continuing to use pastry blender. Shape into a ball. On floured surface, roll dough about ½" thick. Fold in thirds, then shape into a ball again. Repeat rolling 3 times. Wrap and chill several hours or overnight (may also be frozen). Divide dough into 3 parts. Roll out each part into a rectangle ⅛" thick. Cut each rectangle into 12 squares, each 3-4" square. Fill centre of each square with 1 heaping teaspoon of grated apple and ½ tsp. of jam. Bring corners to middle, pinching points together to seal. Place on lightly greased baking sheet. Bake in 400°F oven for 20 minutes, or until golden brown. While still warm, drizzle with a glaze made from icing sugar plus a little milk and vanilla.
Yield: 36

Blintzes   (Jewish)

¾ cup flour, sifted	2 eggs, beaten
½ tsp. salt	⅔ cup milk
1 tsp. baking powder	⅓ cup water
2 tbsp. powdered sugar	½ tsp. vanilla

Resift flour with other dry ingredients. To beaten eggs, add liquids and beat well. Make a well in the flour mixture and pour in liquids. Mix well. Heat a small (5") skillet; grease with a few drops of oil. Add enough batter to cover bottom of pan. Cook over medium heat until brown on bottom and the top bubbles. Remove and place on damp towel. Make up all batter into thin pancakes.

Filling:

1½ cups dry cottage cheese	1 tsp. soft butter
1 egg yolk	1 tsp. vanilla

Garnish:

sugar	heavy cream
cinnamon	

Mix filling ingredients together. Place about 2 tbsp. of filling on each pancake, roll and place seam-side down in a covered dish. These can be cooked immediately, or chilled to cook later. In a large skillet, heat ½ tbsp. oil and ½ tbsp. butter. Place several blintzes in hot mixture, seam-side down. Fry until golden brown, turning once. Repeat, adding more oil and butter until all blintzes are cooked. Serve hot, sprinkled with sugar and cinnamon. Top with heavy cream.

Apfelstrudel (Apple Strudel) (German)

2	cups flour	3	tbsp. cinnamon
2	beaten eggs	6	tbsp. butter, melted
¼	cup lukewarm water	4	tbsp. bread crumbs
	pinch of salt	1	cup chopped almonds
½	tsp. vinegar		(or other nuts)
4-5	lbs. tart apples	1½	cups raisins
⅓	cup sugar		

Heap flour on bread board and make a depression in centre large enough to hold beaten eggs combined with water, salt and vinegar. Knead this to a firm dough which, when cut, will reveal air pockets. Cover dough and set in warm place. Peel, core and grate apples and sprinkle with sugar and cinnamon. Dust a cloth with flour and on it roll out dough, the thinner the better. Melt butter, mix in bread crumbs, and coat dough. Spread apples about 1" high on dough, sprinkle with nuts (optional) and raisins. Roll dough over, in the cloth, several times to form a loaf (strudel) of several alternating layers of dough and filling. Brush finished loaf with more melted butter, place on greased baking sheet. Bake in 400°F oven until crust is crisp and well browned. May be served with vanilla sauce.

Vanillesauce (Vanilla Sauce) (German)

1	cup milk	2	egg yolks
1	tsp. vanilla	½	tsp. cornstarch
1	tbsp. sugar		

Heat milk and vanilla, then cool. Blend sugar, egg yolks and cornstarch until smooth, then stir in milk. Beat in double boiler over moderate heat until mixture thickens. Remove from heat and stir until cool.

Beignettenteig (Beignette Dough) (German)

This basic batter is very versatile. It can be used with a variety of sliced fruit.

2	cups flour	2	tbsp. melted butter
1	egg	1	jigger rum
2	tsp. sugar		warm water
	pinch of salt		fruit of your choice

Mix this batter several hours before serving. Blend all ingredients, except fruit, adding enough warm water to form a creamy batter. Cool. Dip slices of apple, banana, pineapple or other fruits in this sweet batter. Fry in deep hot fat (365°F). Drain on paper towels.

Pjery *(Fruit Dumplings)* (*Czech*)

¼ cup warm water
1 tbsp. sugar
1 tbsp. yeast
3 egg yolks
1 cup warm milk
3 cups flour

fruit (e.g. cherries, strawberries, plums)
sugar
3 tbsp. melted butter
sweetened cottage cheese
sweetened ground poppy seed

Mix warm water, sugar and yeast. Let sit 10 minutes. Mix egg yolks, warm milk, yeast mixture and flour. Beat until smooth. Roll small ball of dough on floured board until flat. Fill with fruit, e.g., cherries, strawberries or plums coated in sugar. Fold dough over filling and seal. Place in boiling water and cover. Boil 5-6 minutes. Take out of water and prick each with fork. Drizzle with melted butter and coat with sweetened cottage cheese or sweetened ground poppy seed.

Babovka (*Czech*)

5 oz. butter
10 oz. icing sugar
5 eggs, beaten
10 oz. flour

2 tsp. baking powder
1 tsp. vanilla sugar
1 cup warm milk
3 tbsp. cocoa

Cream butter and sugar; blend in eggs until smooth. Blend flour, baking powder, vanilla sugar and add alternately with milk. Divide mixture in two. Pour ½ mixture into a doughnut-shaped pan (bundt pan). Add cocoa (if lumpy, sift then add) to remaining mixture, blend until smooth, then pour on top of white batter. Bake in 300°F oven 45-60 minutes.

Thresher's dinner on Siebrasse Farm, Rosyth district, 1913

Eastern Europeans

The Eastern Europeans were a hardy people. They established gardens, diversified their crops and maintained cows and poultry. Even with all the hardships and loneliness they soon realized that immigration to Canada brought a distinct improvement in their standard of living.

1890 – The Austro-Hungarian empire disintegrated. Many groups from Eastern Europe came to North America to escape oppression. The Eastern Europeans that came to Canada were largely impoverished peasants escaping overpopulation, industrial under-development and wealthy landowners that controlled all the land. Ultimately, the vast and fertile tracts of land drew the majority of these immigrants to Western Canada.

Ukrainians – 1901 – The Fourth census in Canada lists Ukrainians as emigrating from Galicia, Russia, Bukovinia, Austria, Ruthenia and Poland.
1892 – The first Ukrainians settled in Alberta with their families. The Ukrainians' inability to speak English often prevented them from taking advantage of the expertise of established English-speaking farmers, who frequently viewed them with hostility and suspicion. Because of their poverty many were forced to work as hired hands for more prosperous farmers. This provided an apprenticeship in techniques of modern farming and generated capital to be invested in land or to be used to send for family members. They had a strong attachment to the land and persisted in farming under difficult environmental circumstances.

Poles – The result of a recruiting campaign by the Canadian government, initiated in Central Europe, brought 115,000 Polish settlers to Canada between 1896-1910. The majority followed their Ukrainian neighbours from Galicia to Western Canada.

Hungarians – 1885 – The First Hungarian colony was established through the efforts of Count Paul D'Esterhazy. A group of Magyars from the U.S. settled near Minnedosa. Great difficulties were encountered, but in 1895 a new influx of settlers came directly from Hungary.

Czechs – The First recorded Czech immigrants to Canada were 4 families that settled in Kolin, Saskatchewan in 1884. Further Czech agriculturists did not come from the Czech lands proper, but from Volhynia (now part of Ukraine) where Czech settlers had been farming for many years.

Romanians – Early settlement was in Boian and Ispas, Alberta. Oppression, a desire to own land and general economics were the main factors influencing their decision to emigrate.

Russians – The first Russians, members of the pacifist Doukabour religious sect, arrived in 1899, 7,000 entered Canada. Apart from the Doukabours, few Russians entered Canada before the first World War.

Greece – Immigration to Canada from Greece began early in the 19th century. The first were seamen who settled in Nova Scotia. Although most preferred large cities, some went into farming in Western Canada.

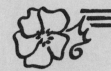

EASTERN EUROPEAN

Mrs. Theresa Ully, outside homestead, Ully, ca. 1915

Rolled Poppyseed Bread   (Ukrainian)

Dough:

2 cups scalded milk (cool to lukewarm)	1 cup granulated sugar
1 tsp. sugar	½ tsp. salt
½ cup lukewarm water	½ cup butter, melted
2 tbsp. yeast	4 eggs, beaten
3 cups flour	6-6½ cups flour

Scald milk and set aside to cool. Dissolve sugar in water; sprinkle in yeast; let stand 10 minutes, then stir well. Stir this mixture into milk. Add flour to yeast, mix well and let rise 1 hour. Stir in sugar, salt, butter and eggs. Add 2 cups of flour to the mixture and mix well. Then add remainder of the flour, mix, and knead 8-10 minutes. Put in greased bowl, cover lightly and let rise 1½ hours. Divide dough into thirds, for 3 loaves. On lightly floured board, roll out each piece of dough into rectangle shape. Spread filling on dough, roll up like jelly roll and place in greased loaf pans. Bake at 325°F for 35-40 minutes.

Filling:

3 egg whites, stiffly beaten	1 lb. ground poppy seeds
½ cup granulated sugar	1 tsp. lemon rind

To prepare filling, beat egg whites, add remaining ingredients and blend lightly.

Gripen Flake (Crackling Bread)   (Russian)

1 cup milk	1 cup cracklings*
2 tsp. baking powder	salt
2 cups flour	

Mix together into a soft dough. Roll out to fit baking sheet. Cut lightly, in squares, but not completely through. Bake in 350°F oven about 30 minutes, until light brown.

* Cracklings are made from freshly ground fat from a hog. They are fried until golden brown.

Nachynka (Spoon Bread)   (Ukrainian)

1 small onion, finely chopped	¼ tsp. pepper
3 tbsp. butter	¼ tsp. cinnamon
1 cup cornmeal	3½ cups scalded milk
1 tsp. sugar	½ cup light cream
1 tsp. salt	3 eggs, well beaten

In saucepan, sauté onion in butter until tender, not brown. Add cornmeal, sugar and seasonings; mix well. Gradually pour in scalded milk; stir briskly until smooth. Cook until mixture thickens. Remove from heat, blend in cream, then fold in eggs. Pour into 8" cake pan or casserole and bake, uncovered, in 350°F oven 50- 60 minutes, until golden.

Paska (Easter Bread)   (Ukrainian)

1 cup light cream	5-5½ cups flour, divided
¾ cup sugar	4 eggs, beaten
½ cup butter	2 tsp. vanilla
½ tsp. salt	1 tbsp. grated lemon rind
2 pkgs. dry yeast	

Scald cream in small saucepan. Stir in sugar, butter and salt until butter melts. Set aside in pan and cool to lukewarm. In large bowl mix yeast and 1½ cups flour. Gradually add cream mixture and beat until smooth. Add eggs, vanilla, lemon rind and 1 cup flour, again beating until smooth. Gradually stir in more flour to make soft dough. Shape dough into a ball on lightly floured board. Flour hands and knead dough, turning and folding, adding just enough flour to keep dough from sticking. Dough should be smooth and elastic. Form into ball and place in large greased bowl, turning to grease all over. Cover and set in warm place about 1½ hours, until double in size. Punch dough down, then place on lightly floured board for 5 minutes. Cut into 2 parts to make wreaths.

Wreaths:
Take the 2 parts and divide each into 3 parts, rolling each like a rope. Braid 3 ropes and form into a wreath. Put 4 or 5 uncooked eggs, in the shell, in the centre of each wreath and press into dough. Cover and let rise to double in size, about 1½ hours. Before baking, remove eggs, brush dough with glaze, replace eggs in depressions. Bake in 350°F oven 35 minutes. Remove hot eggs, colour or decorate eggs and, when bread is cool, place back in depressions in wreath.

Glaze:

1 egg, beaten	1 tbsp. milk

Mix and drizzle over wreaths.

Avgolemono *(Egg and Lemon Soup)* (Greek)

A classic Greek recipe.

6 cups chicken broth	2 egg yolks
⅓ cup uncooked rice	1 lemon, juice of

Heat broth to boiling point, add rice and simmer 30 minutes, until rice is tender. Beat yolks and lemon juice until frothy. Gradually add 1 cup of the broth, blend well, then pour all lemon mixture back into rest of the soup, stirring constantly with wire whisk. Reheat, but do not boil, and serve. Yield: 6 servings.

Cold Borscht (Russian)

1 lb. raw beets, peeled, grated	2 eggs, beaten
1 qt. water	sour cream
salt and pepper	2 hard-boiled eggs, sliced
lemon juice	1 cucumber, sliced
sugar	

Cook beets in salt water until tender. Add pepper, lemon juice and sugar to give sweet/sour taste. Taste soup to see if there is enough salt. Chill. Beat eggs in large bowl, add borscht, return to pot and heat slowly (do not boil), stirring constantly until slightly thickened. Chill well before serving. Garnish each serving with sour cream, hard-boiled eggs and cucumber.

Borscht (Russian)

1 cup chopped onion	1 cup peeled, grated beets
1 tbsp. finely chopped garlic	4 cups shredded red cabbage
1 tbsp. butter	1 tsp. caraway seeds
10 cups beef stock (fat skimmed off)	1 tsp. sugar (optional)
2 cups chopped ripe tomatoes	2 tbsp. lemon juice

In soup kettle, briefly sauté onion and garlic in butter for 2-3 minutes. Stirring constantly, add stock and rest of ingredients. Bring just to the boil, reduce heat and simmer 90 minutes. Stir occasionally. Serve hot.

Ukranian Cuisine

In Ukraine, cooking is considered an art. Great emphasis is always placed on palatability of food. Ukranian dishes are neither highly spiced nor bland – they are subtle and pleasing, having their own indefinable qualities.

In Ukraine, a meal would be incomplete without a soup course. Be the family rich or poor, soup is a daily "must". Soup never boils with a full, rollicking boil, but simmers gently for hours. Borsch, with its many variations, is the most popular as well as the national soup of Ukraine.

Standard Borsch

This recipe for Borsch is the most commonly used – with slight variations. For a well-flavored Borsch, it is best to use some fresh lean pork and a small piece of smoked pork, along with beef, for the broth base.

1½ lbs. soup meat with bones	2-3 cups shredded cabbage
10-12 cups cold water	⅔ cup strained tomatoes or tomato juice
1 tsp. salt	
1 medium onion, chopped	½ garlic clove, crushed
2 medium beets, cut in thin strips	1 tbsp. flour
1 small carrot, cut in thin strips	3 tbsp. cold water
1 medium potato, diced	lemon juice
½ cup thinly sliced celery	salt and pepper
½ cup diced string beans or cooked white beans	½ cup sour cream chopped dill

Cover meat with cold water, add salt, bring slowly to boiling point. Skim off scum. Cover and simmer 1½ hours. Add onions and beets; cook 10-15 minutes or until beets are almost done. Add carrot, potato, celery, string beans; continue cooking about 10 minutes. When cooked white beans are used, add after cabbage is cooked. Add cabbage, cook until tender. Stir in tomatoes, or juice, and garlic. Blend flour with cold water, spoon into it some soup liquid, then stir into Borsch. Add lemon juice to taste. A good borsch should be pleasantly tart but not sour. Season to taste with salt and pepper; bring to boiling point. When ready to serve, add some thick sour cream or rich sweet cream. Cream can be put into each individual serving, if preferred. Garnish with chopped dill.

Variation: Two medium beets may be replaced by more small beets, with tops.

Dumbwaiter – A stacked shelf, lowered, usually with ropes, through the floor into the cellar, to keep food cool.

Kapusnyak (*Sauerkraut Soup*) (*Ukranian*)

½ lb. smoked pork shank or
    fresh spareribs
8 cups water
1 medium onion, chopped
1 medium potato, diced
1 small carrot, sliced
½ cup chopped mushrooms

3 cups sauerkraut
1 tbsp. finely chopped onion
1 tbsp. fat
2 tbsp. flour
1 tbsp. sour cream
  salt and pepper
  chopped dill or parsley

Wash meat, cover with water, simmer until tender. Add more water if needed. Add onion, potato, carrot; simmer until done. Remove meat and press vegetables through a sieve. Return meat and pressed vegetable stock to kettle; add mushrooms and sauerkraut. Simmer until kraut is tender, about 20 minutes. Cook onion in hot fat until tender, stir in flour and brown lightly. Pour in some soup liquid, stir until smooth, add to soup. Add sour cream, season to taste and bring to boil. Flavor with dill or parsley. Serve meat as separate course, or place a small portion in each bowl. This soup is usually served with rye bread.

Cabbage Borscht with Barley (*Ukranian*)

1-2 lbs. beef soup bones
2 qts. water
½ cup pot barley
1 head cabbage, coarsely cut
1 carrot, shredded
2 large onions, diced

1 large bay leaf
8 peppercorns
1 bunch parsley
1 bunch dill
1 qt. stewed tomatoes
  sweet cream

Bring soup bones and water to boil. Skim off scum. Add barley and simmer about 2 hours, until barley is nearly done. Add cabbage, carrots and onions. Bring back to boil and add spices, parsley and dill. Simmer until vegetables are tender. Add tomatoes and simmer 10 minutes. Add cream and serve. To vary, omit barley.

Cabbage Soup (*Hungarian*)

1½ lbs. pork spareribs
5 bay leaves
4 qts. water
5 tbsp. oil
1 tsp. caraway seeds
1 large green cabbage

5 peppercorns
2 tbsp. salt
5 tbsp. flour
6 cups tomato juice
1 tbsp. sugar

In a large pot, cook spareribs and bay leaves in water for about 1½ hours. Heat 3 tbsp. oil in a heavy large casserole; add caraway seeds, then add shredded cabbage. (Cut cabbage by hand.) Add peppercorns and salt; sauté for about 40 minutes, until cabbage is cooked. Heat 2 tbsp. oil in a pot, add flour, make a light brown roux. Then add tomato juice and sugar, cook for about 5 minutes, until bubbling. To assemble, add tomato roux to cooked cabbage, then add cooked spareribs and liquid. Salt to taste. Simmer for 10 more minutes. Serve with good rye bread. Yield: 8 servings.

Csontle (*Soup Stock*)   (*Hungarian*)

4-5	soup bones	10	peppercorns
5-6	cups meat scraps (beef, veal, pork)	1	slice fresh ginger
3-4	qts. water	1	onion, sliced
1	tsp. salt	1	garlic clove, minced

Place all ingredients in a large kettle. Simmer gently for several hours. Strain to clear. Cool. Use for various soups and other dishes.

Bableves Rantva (*Bean Soup*)   (*Hungarian*)

2	cups dry beans	1	medium onion, chopped
6	cups water	2	tbsp. oil
	smoked meat (sausage or knuckles)	1	tsp. paprika
1	tbsp. salt	1	cup sour cream
2	carrots, sliced		Csipelke (pinched noodles),
1	parsnip, sliced		page 134

Soak beans overnight, drain, rinse with cold water, drain. To beans add 6 cups water, meat and salt. Cook slowly 1½ hours. Add vegetables and cook until tender. Make pinched noodles and add to boiling soup, cooking until tender. Stir in sour cream just before serving.

Mr. & Mrs. D. Bilej, from Romania, Shandro, 1903

Csipelke *(Pinched Noodles)* *(Hungarian)*

1 egg
parsley, minced, to taste (optional)
salt to taste
flour

Combine ingredients with enough flour to make medium dough. Drop tiny noodles from spoon into simmering soup. When they rise to top test for doneness.

Gyumolcs Leves *(Fruit Soup)* *(Hungarian)*

1 lb. fruit (cherries, apples,
   red currants
1 qt. water
1 lemon, juice and grated rind
2 tbsp. flour

¾ cup heavy cream
½ cup sugar
¼ cup butter
1 cup red wine (optional)

Prepare fruit as required: wash, peel, core, slice apples or pit cherries. Boil water with lemon juice. Add prepared fruit and let simmer. Mix paste of flour and cream, add to fruit mixture. Bring to boil. Add sugar, grated lemon rind, butter and red wine, if using. Serve hot.

Zoldborsoleves *(Green Pea Soup)* *(Hungarian)*

1 small onion, minced
2 tbsp. fat
1 tsp. paprika
1 lb. fresh garden peas
2 carrots, diced

1 tomato, diced
½ green pepper, diced
sprigs of parsley
1 tsp. flour
soup stock

Sauté onion in fat until golden. Remove from heat, stir in paprika. Add vegetables, sauté 10 minutes. Sprinkle with flour. Add desired amount of soup stock. Cook until vegetables are tender. Serve with Nokedli, below.

Nokedli *(Dumplings)* *(Hungarian)*

butter or shortening, size of walnut
1 egg
salt to taste

3-4 tbsp. water or milk
flour to make medium-soft dough

Combine ingredients, drop from a teaspoon into soup. Cook 2-3 minutes and serve.

Pea Soup with Noodles   *(Hungarian)*

2 tbsp. oil	2 carrots, diced
1 medium onion	½ cup parsley
2 tsp. paprika	salt and pepper
4-5 cups peas	8 cups water

Heat oil. Add chopped onion and sauté. Add paprika and stir to coat onions. Add peas, carrots and parsley. Add salt and pepper; stir and add boiling water. Simmer about ½ hour. While soup is cooking make noodles, below. This quantity of noodles makes a very thick soup. If you like a soup with more broth make only half the recipe of noodles.

Grated Noodles:

2 eggs	1 tsp. salt
¼ cup water	3-3½ cups flour

Beat eggs lightly. Stir in water and salt. Add 2 cups of the flour and stir until smooth. Add remaining flour, gradually, working it in well. The dough should be stiff enough to grate on the largest holes of a grater. Try grating after adding the third cup of flour. If dough is not stiff enough, add remaining flour, a little at a time. Grate noodles. While soup is boiling, add noodles, stirring so that noodles don't lump together. Cook about 5 minutes.

Sorrel Soup   *(Hungarian)*

1 ham bone	5 medium potatoes, diced
2½ cups water	1 bay leaf
3 cups finely chopped sorrel leaves or beet greens	½ cup cream (sweet or sour)
1 cup chopped green onions	salt to taste

Cook ham bone in water for 1 hour. Remove and add vegetables and bay leaf to stock. Simmer until potatoes are cooked. Add cream and salt just before serving.

Karfoil Leves *(Cauliflower Soup)*   *(Hungarian)*

1 small onion, minced	1 medium cauliflower, sliced or cubed
2 tbsp. fat	1-2 smoked sausages, sliced
1 tsp. paprika	1 qt. soup stock
1 carrot, diced	2 tbsp. flour
1 parsnip, diced	¼ cup milk

In saucepan, sauté onion in fat. Remove from heat; stir in paprika, carrots and parsnips; return to heat and sauté 10 minutes. Add cauliflower, sausage and stock. Simmer until vegetables are tender. Blend flour with milk and thicken to desired consistency. Do not overcook. Serve hot.

Csireke Porkolt *(Chicken Paprika)* *(Hungarian)*

3 lb. chicken, in pieces	3 tbsp. shortening
salt and pepper	2 tbsp. paprika
2 medium onions, minced	1 tbsp. tomato purée
1 green pepper, minced	1 cup water
1 tomato, chopped	

Season chicken with salt and pepper. Sauté vegetables in shortening until golden brown. Add chicken pieces, sauté 30 minutes. Remove from heat, stir in paprika. Let stand several minutes, then add tomato purée and water. Cover and cook 15 minutes more, or until chicken is tender. Place chicken pieces on serving dish. Remove vegetables and press through sieve. Stir back into sauce, then pour over chicken. Garnish with sliced raw vegetables, if desired. Serve with Galuska (Little Dumplings), below.

Galuska *(Little Dumplings)* *(Hungarian)*

2 cups flour	2 tbsp. fat
¾ cups water	1 tsp. salt
2 eggs	

Blend all ingredients to form dough. Place a portion of dough on wet bread board. Cut into narrow strips with wet knife, then cut strips into small pieces and place in salted boiling water. Stir and wait until these mini dumplings come to surface. Place in heat-proof dish, dot with butter. Cook remaining noodles the same way. Serve with Csirke Porkolt (Chicken Paprika), above, or Bacska Steak with Lecso, page 137.

Gypsy Cure-All

10 cents of linseed – boil like molasses
10 cents rock sugar
5 cents of white wine vinegar
½ dozen lemons – roast in oven
A little brandy

Mix together – take a teaspoonful every day.

Bacska Steak with Lecsa   *(Hungarian)*

1 tsp. salt
5 steaks (6 oz. ea.)
1 tsp. flour
⅓ cup lard
1 oz. chopped onion
1 tsp. paprika

1 tsp. tomato purée
2 garlic cloves, crushed
   caraway seed
   marjoram
5 oz. Lecsa, below

Salt steaks, dredge with flour. Fry both sides quickly in lard. Remove from pan. Fry onions until golden brown; add remaining ingredients, except Lecsa. Add ½ cup water, boil 5 minutes. Return steaks to pan and add water to cover. Simmer slowly, turning occasionally, adding water to keep covered. When meat is nearly tender, add Lecsa, then continue cooking until tender. May be served with a layer of Galuska (Little Dumplings), page 136, over each steak. Yield: 5 servings.

Lesca   *(Hungarian)*

1/4 cup smoked bacon, chopped
2 tbsp. finely chopped onion
1 tsp. paprika

3 large tomatoes, quartered
   salt
2 green peppers, sliced

Fry bacon on medium heat, 5 minutes. Add onion, sauté until golden. Add paprika, tomatoes and salt to taste. Simmer, covered, on medium heat until tomatoes are stewed, about 10 minutes. Add sliced green peppers and cook until peppers are just tender.

Paprikas *(Paprika Beef Stew)*   *(Hungarian)*

2 tbsp. lard
2 onions, chopped
2 tbsp. paprika

3 lbs. stewing beef, cut in 2" pieces
1 tsp. salt
2 carrots

Heat lard in a heavy pot. Add chopped onion and sauté. Add paprika and stir to blend. Add cubed meat and salt and stir until all meat is coated. Be careful that the meat does not scorch. Cover and cook over medium-low heat stirring frequently until juices begin to form. When liquid has formed, reduce heat to simmer and cook until meat is tender, 2-3 hours. A little water can also be added after the meat has cooked for a while, if you want more juice. While adding vegetables is not traditional, the carrots add colour without altering the flavour.

Tomatoes – Taken from the Andes region of South America to Europe in the 16th Century, they were used in Mediterranean countries and have been cultivated in the U.S. since the 1700s. Not until the 19th Century were tomatoes accepted in Northern regions – they were feared to be poisonous!

Roc Hol *(Baked Whitefish)* *(Hungarian)*

3-4 lb. whitefish
    salt and pepper
4 medium, potatoes, peeled,
    boiled, sliced
1 green pepper, sliced
3-4 tomatoes, sliced

1 tsp. flour
1 tsp. paprika
4-6 slices bacon, fried
    and crumbled
2 cups sour cream
2 tbsp. butter, melted

Fillet fish, soak, wash, dry thoroughly. Salt and pepper to taste. Arrange layer of potatoes on bottom of greased baking dish. Add layer of green pepper and half of tomatoes. Season with salt and pepper. Place fish on top. Sprinkle with flour, paprika and bacon bits. Spread rest of tomatoes over, then pour over sour cream. Bake in 400°F oven 15 minutes, then pour melted butter over and bake 15 minutes more, until fish is tender.

Hutterites, Rockyford area, 1919

Paprikasburgonya *(Potatoes with Paprika)* *(Hungarian)*

2-3 onions, finely chopped
    lard or fat
1¼ tsp. paprika

6-8 large potatoes, peeled, diced small
    salt
½ cup sour cream

Lightly brown onions in fat. Mix in paprika, add potatoes and salt to taste. Simmer gently; add hot water occasionally until potatoes are tender, but not too soft. Stir in sour cream 5 minutes before serving.

Varenyky (Filled Dumplings)   (Ukranian)

For most red-blooded Ukrainians, no dish is more tempting to feast on than well-filled plump Varenyky made of soft dough and served with a generous portion of "smetana" (sour cream). Fillings for Varenyky are numerous, but cottage cheese is the national favorite.

Dough Preparation and Cooking Method:

2 cups flour	1 tbsp. melted fat
½ cup cold mashed potatoes	1 egg or 2 egg yolks
1 tsp. salt	½ cup or more cold water

Mix flour with mashed potato, salt and fat. Add egg and enough water to make a soft dough. Knead on floured board until smooth. Too much kneading will toughen dough. Divide into 2 parts, cover and let stand at least 10 minutes. Roll dough quite thin on floured board. Cut in rounds or 2-2½" squares. Put round or square on palm of hand, place spoonful of filling (filling recipes follow) on dough, fold over to form half-circle or triangle, press edges together with fingers. Be sure edges are sealed well to prevent filling running out. Place on floured board without crowding. Cover. Drop a few at a time into a large quantity of rapidly boiling salted water. Stir gently to separate and prevent sticking. Continue boiling rapidly, 3-4 minutes, until well puffed. Remove to colander and drain thoroughly. Place in deep dish, sprinkle with melted butter, coating evenly, to prevent sticking. Serve with sour cream, browned buttered bread crumbs, chopped crisp bacon or chopped onion lightly browned in butter, or a combination of any of these toppings.

Potato and Cheese Filling:

Mashed, seasoned potatoes may be used alone as a filling for Varenyky, but the addition of cheese gives it a superior flavor. Cottage cheese, grated Cheddar or cream cheese makes an excellent combination with mashed potatoes.

1 tbsp. onion, grated	1 cup cottage cheese (or other
2 tbsp. butter	cheeses)
2 cups cold mashed potatoes	salt and pepper to taste

Cook onion in butter until tender. Combine with potatoes and cheese. Season with salt and pepper.

Sauerkraut Filling:

Varenyky with sauerkraut filling are always served at the Christmas Eve supper, but may be served any time of year.

3 cups sauerkraut	2 tbsp. sour cream
1 medium onion, chopped	salt and pepper
4 tbsp. butter	

Rinse sauerkraut well in warm water, squeeze dry, chop very fine. Cook onion in butter until tender. Add kraut, cream, salt and pepper to taste. Cook over low heat 15 minutes, or until kraut is tender. Do not overcook. Chill before using.

Alternative: Fill dumplings with strawberries, raspberries or chopped apricots.

Beet Leaf Holubtsi   (Ukrainian)

2   cups cold water
1   cup rice
¼   tsp. salt
¼   cup chopped onions
½   cup butter

⅛   cup chopped dill
    salt and pepper
½   cup cream
    beet leaves

Bring water, rice and salt to a boil, cover and steam 10 minutes on low heat. Fry onions in butter until onions are translucent. Add to rice along with dill, salt and pepper. Pick young, fresh beet leaves; wilt them in oven at 200°F or pour boiling water over and drain. Place 1 tsp. rice mixture on each beet leaf; fold sides over filling and roll tightly. Place in layers in baking dish or casserole. Pour cream over Holubtsi; cover and bake at 300°F ½-¾ hour.

Baked Chicken with Cream   (Ukrainian)

A favourite Sunday dinner in many Ukrainian homes.

3-4   lb. chicken
      salt
      pepper

1   tbsp. flour
1   cup whipping cream
1   medium onion

Cut chicken, rinse and place in a baking pan. Season with salt and pepper. Cover and bake at 325°F for about ½ hour. Remove from oven and skim off drippings. Blend the flour with a small amount of water to make a smooth paste. Combine with cream. Chop onion and sprinkle over chicken. Pour cream mixture over. Return to oven and bake for ½ hour, or until chicken is lightly browned.

Toltolt Kaposzta (Cabbage Rolls)   (Hungarian)

1   medium cabbage
1   tsp. salt
1   tbsp. vinegar
1½   lbs. ground pork
½   lb. ground beef
½   cup rice, partially cooked
2   eggs
      salt and pepper

1   medium onion, finely chopped
28   oz. sauerkraut
5   tbsp. lard
3   tbsp. flour
2   tsp. paprika
1   cup cold water
½   cup sour cream
½   cup whipping cream

Remove core of cabbage. Cover with boiling water, salt and vinegar. Simmer few minutes then cool. Mix meat, rice, eggs, salt, pepper, onion. Separate cabbage leaves. Use small leaves and cut larger leaves in half. Place 2 tbsp. meat mixture in each leaf, roll a little, tuck ends in and roll up tightly. Drain sauerkraut, put half in large pot. Place cabbage rolls side by side on top of sauerkraut. Cover with remaining sauerkraut. Pour 2 cups boiling water over, bring to a boil, reduce heat and simmer 1 hour. Brown lard and flour, add paprika and 1 cup cold water. Bring mixture to boil, pour over cabbage rolls. Simmer another ½ hour, being careful not to burn on bottom. Serve with a mixture of sour cream and whipping cream. Yield: 6-8 servings.

Lamb Tokany with Green Peas *(Hungarian)*

2 lbs. lamb shoulder, cut in
   2" strips
5 oz. onions, finely chopped
3½ oz. lard
1 garlic clove, crushed

1 tsp. tomato purée
2 tbsp. dry white wine
   or clear soup stock
   salt and pepper
2 cups fresh green peas

Prepare meat. Fry onion in lard until golden. Add garlic, tomato purée and wine. Boil 5 minutes. Add meat, salt and pepper, cover and simmer until meat is tender. Add peas, bring to boil. Do not overcook peas. If too thick, add a little water. Yield: 5-6 servings.

Suggestion: Serve with rice or mashed potatoes.

Ragoût of Lamb   *(Romanian)*

2½ lbs. lamb shoulder
1 onion, chopped
3 tbsp. butter
1 tsp. flour
2 cups stewed tomatoes
2 cups stock

   salt and pepper
2 lbs. string beans
½ cup white wine
6 medium potatoes, boiled
2 tbsp. chopped parsley

Wipe meat dry, then cut into 1" cubes. In skillet, sauté meat and onion in melted butter until light brown. Make paste of flour and 1 tsp. cold water and add to pan. Stir in tomatoes and stock, and season to taste. Wash beans, remove strings, pile over meat mixture. Add wine. Cover and simmer about 1 hour, until meat is tender. Serve hot with cooked potatoes, sprinkled with parsley.

Tocana Ciobanului Cu Varza   *(Romanian)*
(Shepherd's Sauerkraut Stew)

4 large onions, chopped
   bacon drippings
   salt and pepper
2 lbs. sauerkraut

2 lbs. pork or spareribs
1 cup sour cream
   paprika, dill, thyme

Cook onions in 3 tbsp. drippings until soft. Add salt and pepper to taste. Rinse sauerkraut in cold water; squeeze out excess liquid; add to pan of onions and fry 10 minutes. Cut meat into cubes. Place in separate large pan with a tight cover. Sear quickly until browned. Add onions and sauerkraut to meat, add 1 cup cold water, cover and cook slowly 30 minutes. When almost done, add sour cream, generous dash paprika, dill and thyme; mix well. Cook 5 minutes. Cover and let stand 1 hour, until flavours penetrate mixture. Reheat just before serving.

Suggestion: Serve with baked potatoes and side vegetables.

Dolmathes *(Stuffed Grape Leaves)* (Greek)

40 fresh grape leaves or 9-oz. jar of grape leaves

Filling:

1½	lbs. ground beef	½-¾	cup cooked rice
1	large onion, grated		salt and pepper
3	tbsp. butter		
2	tsp. chopped parsley, or mint or 1 tsp. of each		

Broth:

2 cups chicken or beef broth

Parboil grape leaves 5 minutes. If using canned leaves, drain and rinse thoroughly.

Place meat in bowl. Sauté onion in butter and add to meat, along with rest of ingredients. Mix well. To fill leaves: Keep shiny side of leaf on outside. Place spoonful of filling on each leaf, fold sides over, then roll. (Use 2 leaves overlapped if leaves are small). Line pan with a few leaves; carefully arrange Dolmathes in layers.

Pour broth over Dolmathes and simmer 1 hour, or until done. Drain just before serving (reserving 1 cup of liquid for sauce, below). Serve with Avgolemono Saltsa (Egg Lemon Sauce).

Avgolemono Saltsa *(Egg Lemon Sauce)* (Greek)

3	eggs, well beaten	1	cup liquid from Dolmathes
2	lemons, juice of		

Beat eggs until light and fluffy. Slowly blend in lemon juice. Place in double boiler. Gradually add hot, but not boiling, Dolmathes liquid, beating constantly. Pour sauce evenly over drained Dolmathes, and serve.

Recipe for Rural Progress

Take a large measure of foresight, good judgment and clear thinking.
Add a desire to work with neighbours for mutual advantage.
Mix well with a quantity of cooperative education.
Keep out all petty spite and jealousies.
Pour in a goodly measure of the milk of human kindness.
Spice with a desire for the advancement of fellow humans.
Mix well together.
Result: Success and cooperation.

Moussaka   *(Middle Eastern)*

2   lbs. eggplant
    salt
1   tbsp. oil
½-¾ cup grated Parmesan cheese
1   medium onion, chopped
2   garlic cloves, finely chopped
2   tbsp. olive oil
1-2 lbs. ground beef or lamb
1   cup tomatoes, chopped
2   tbsp. tomato paste

½   cup red or white wine
2   tbsp. chopped parsley
    salt and pepper to taste
½   tsp. ground oregano
¼   tsp. cinnamon or nutmeg
½-1 tsp. sugar
3   tbsp. butter
3   tbsp. flour
1½-2 cups milk
2   large egg yolks, beaten,
    or 1-2 eggs, beaten

Lightly grease shallow 2-quart casserole. Wash eggplant, do not peel, cut into ½" slices, salt well and set aside for 1 hour to drain. Wipe dry, brush with oil, broil 2-3 minutes each side and place 1 layer in casserole. Sprinkle with ¼ cup Parmesan. In large saucepan, sauté onion and garlic in olive oil until soft. Add meat, cook until no longer pink, drain and add tomatoes, tomato paste, wine, seasonings and sugar. Simmer 15 minutes. Spread over eggplant and cheese, sprinkle another ¼ cup cheese over mixture and a layer of remaining eggplant. In saucepan, melt butter, stir in flour, cook 1 minute. Add milk and stir until thickened. Mix a little sauce into egg yolks (or eggs), then stir into sauce and pour over eggplant. Sprinkle remaining cheese over all. Bake in 375°F oven, uncovered, 30-35 minutes.

Kapusta *(Sauerkraut)*   *(Polish)*

1   oz. dried mushrooms
½   cup warm water
3   tbsp. butter
1   large onion, diced
1   medium tomato, diced
2   lbs. sauerkraut, rinsed and drained

1   cup dry white wine
½   cup beef stock
½   tsp. salt
⅛   tsp. pepper
2   tbsp. flour
    pinch of sugar

Soak mushrooms in water for ½ hour, then drain, saving liquid. Chop mushrooms and sauté in butter. Add onion and tomato and sauté until onion is translucent. Add sauerkrat, wine, stock, mushroom water, salt and pepper ans simmer. Sprinkle flour over sauerkraut mixture; stir in, and simmer, covered, 30 minutes, stirring occasionally. Add a pinch of sugar and serve.
Yield. 4-6 servings.

Honey Cake   (Greek)

4 eggs, separated	2 oranges, juice and grated rind
½ cup sugar	1 cup honey
1 cup cream of wheat	1 lemon, juice of

Beat egg yolks, add sugar, beat until lemon-coloured. Add cream of wheat alternately with orange juice and rind. Fold in stiffly beaten egg whites. Pour in 8" square pan. Bake at 350°F for 20-25 minutes. Cool 5 minutes. Blend honey and lemon juice. Bring to boil, simmer 1 minute. Drizzle evenly over warm cake.

Homemade Honey

Making honey without bees goes back about 300 years. When gathering clover, watch for 4-leafed ones. Seeing one brings good luck – picking it brings grief!

10 cups sugar	5 fragrant rose petals
3 cups water	40 red clover blossoms
½ tsp. powdered alum	80 white clover blossoms

Combine first 3 ingredients and boil 5 minutes. Pour over petals and blossoms, let stand 20 minutes. Strain through cheesecloth into jar. Store in a dry place.

Rice Pudding   (Greek)

⅔ cup water	½ cup sugar
pinch of salt	1 orange or lemon, grated peel of
½ cup rice	1 tsp. vanilla
4 cups milk	seedless grapes
4 egg yolks, beaten	cinnamon

Bring water to boil in covered pan. Add salt and rice, cover and cook 4 minutes on medium heat. Remove from heat; keep covered. Scald milk in large pot, then stir in cooked rice. Cook over low heat about 35 minutes, stirring occasionally. Remove from heat. Cream egg yolks with sugar; stir into rice. Stir in grated peel. Cook and stir constantly over low heat until thick and creamy. Remove from heat; stir in vanilla. In a large bowl or individual bowls, decorate with grapes, sprinkle with cinnamon and chill. Yield: 6 servings.

Szilvas Gomboc *(Plum Dumplings)* *(Hungarian)*

4 baking potatoes	2 lbs. plums (or apricots)
2 egg yolks	sugar cubes
1 tsp. salt	buttered bread crumbs
1 tbsp. butter	sugar
2 cups flour (approx.)	cinnamon

Boil potatoes in skins. Peel, mash and chill. Mix in egg yolks, salt and butter. Add half of flour and knead, adding more flour as needed until dough is smooth and resilient. Roll into long sausage-like rolls, about 1" diameter. Slice into 1½" pieces. Cut fruit just enough to remove pits, replace pit with sugar cube and press together. Wrap dough around fruit and press edges to seal. Cook in rapidly boiling water for 15 minutes, or until dumplings rise to surface. Reduce heat and simmer 10 minutes longer. Remove with slotted spoon; drain. Roll in bread crumbs browned in butter. Sprinkle with sugar and cinnamon, if desired. Serves 6.

Russian Settlers, Unity, Saskatchewan, n.d.

Dobos Torte (Hungarian)

This famous torte was named after Jozef C. Dobos, born in 1847. He sold this delicious cake in his fabulous specialty food shop in Budapest.

9 eggs, separated	2 cups powdered sugar
⅛ tsp. salt	1 cup less 3 tbsp. flour

In a large bowl, beat egg whites with salt until stiff, but not dry. Beat in ½ cup powdered sugar, a little at a time, until sugar dissolves and whites become glossy. Beat egg yolks with remaining sugar until thick and lemon-coloured. Gently fold yolk mixture into egg whites, along with flour, until well blended. Lightly grease and dust with flour 10, 8" layer pans, if you have them. Otherwise, bake in 2 or 3 equal portions at a time, keeping batter cool until all used. Pour equal portions of batter into prepared pans. Bake in 375°F oven 12-15 minutes, or until light brown. Cake should spring back to touch of finger. Carefully turn out on waxed paper sprinkled with sugar. Cool. Layers should be about ¼" thick.

Butter Cream and Chocolate Filling:

1 cup plus 3 tbsp. soft butter	3 egg yolks, unbeaten
2 cups powdered sugar	8 oz. semisweet chocolate bits

Beat butter until fluffy; gradually add sugar, then egg yolks, 1 at a time, beating until very fluffy. Melt and cool chocolate; blend into butter mixture. Cool if too soft. Spread generously on 9 layers, place one on top of the other. Do not spread on top layer.

Caramel Topping:

⅔ cup granulated sugar	¼ tsp. cream of tartar
⅓ cup water	

Put in a small saucepan and bring to a boil, stirring until bubbles disappear. Spread on top layer, working quickly, then spread around sides of cake. Keep cool.

Dobos Torta (Variation) (Hungarian)

Cake:

¾ cup sugar	7 tbsp. flour
7 eggs, separated	½ tsp. baking powder

Beat sugar and egg yolks well. Mix flour and baking powder and add to sugar mixture. Slowly fold stiffly beaten egg whites into sugar mixture. Pour batter thinly into 6 greased 8" cake pans cake pans. Bake in 350°F oven 5 minutes.

Mocha Icing:

½ lb. butter (1 cup)	¼ cup cocoa
1 egg yolk	1 tsp. vanilla
1-2 tsp. strong coffee	1 lb. powdered sugar

Beat all ingredients together until creamy. Frost each layer, placing one on top of the other, and frost top of entire cake. Decorate if desired.

Coffee Cake   (Hungarian)

1 tsp. sugar	⅓ cup sugar
1 pkg. yeast	1½ tsp. salt
¼ cup lukewarm water	1 cup water
1½ cups milk	6 eggs, beaten
3 tbsp. butter	8 cups flour

Walnut Raisin Filling:

¼ cup melted butter	½ cup raisins
1 cup brown sugar	2 tsp. cinnamon
1 cup chopped walnuts	

Dissolve 1 tsp. sugar in lukewarm water; add yeast and let stand 10 minutes. Scald milk, add butter, sugar and salt and stir until dissolved. Add water and cool to lukewarm. Add eggs and yeast mixture and stir well. Add flour gradually to make soft dough. Knead well until dough is smooth and elastic. Place in buttered bowl. Cover with a towel and let stand in warm place until doubled in bulk, approximately 1 hour. Punch down and shape.

To make a cake, pinch off small bits of dough, about 1" across, and roll into balls. Dip balls in melted butter and roll in sugar and nuts. Place close together in deep buttered pan. When a layer is made, sprinkle raisins over and make another layer, repeating all steps until pan is a little more than half full. Let rise until doubled. Bake at 350°F for 40-50 minutes.

Hungarian Slice   (Hungarian)

Base:

½ cup brown sugar	1 tsp. salt
1 cup butter	2 eggs, separated
1½ cups flour	1 tsp. vanilla
1½ tsp. baking powder	

Brown Sugar Topping:

1 cup nuts, chopped	1 cup brown sugar
2 egg whites, stiffly beaten	

Cream sugar and butter, blend in dry ingredients. Beat yolks lightly with vanilla and add to batter. Save whites for topping. Pat batter evenly in 8" pan. Bake in very slow oven (250°F) ½ hour.

Remove base from oven. Sprinkle nuts on base. Blend brown sugar in beaten egg whites. Spread over nuts. Return to oven until topping is lightly browned.

Makos Kalacs *(Poppy Seed Roll)* *(Hungarian)*

1 pkg. yeast	2 tsp. salt
2 tsp. sugar	½ cup butter, melted
½ cup lukewarm water	½ cup milk, scalded
3 eggs, well beaten	½ cup water
½ cup sugar	flour to make soft dough

Combine yeast, sugar and lukewarm water. Let stand 10 minutes. Beat eggs, sugar, salt and butter. Combine scalded milk and water and add to egg mixture. Make certain mixture is not too hot before adding yeast mixture. Add flour gradually, mixing well to make a soft dough. Knead until elastic. Place in greased bowl. Cover and let rise until double. Punch down and roll out to ¼" thick. Spread with poppy seed filling and roll like a jelly roll. Place in greased pan and let rise again until doubled. Bake at 375°F for 35-40 minutes.

Poppy Seed Filling:

8 oz. poppy seeds, ground	½-¾ cup whipping cream
1-1½ cups sugar	1 tsp. vanilla
½ cup raisins, washed	

To make filling, combine poppy seeds with 1 cup sugar, raisins and cream in heavy pot. Simmer over low heat for 10 minutes. Taste. If not sweet enough add remaining sugar. Simmer until mixture thickens. Add vanilla. Cool slightly before filling poppy seed roll.

Ara Strambouli *(Pumpkin Dessert)* *(Turkish)*

1 small pumpkin, peeled, sliced	1 cup currants
½ cup butter or shortening	lemon juice (approx. juice of
1 cup chopped nuts	1 lemon for each layer)
1 cup sugar	¼ cup rum

Slowly fry pumpkin in butter until tender; drain and place in layers in shallow baking dish. Mix nuts, sugar and currants with enough juice to moisten sugar. Spread on each layer of pumpkin; top layer is pumpkin. Pour rum over all. Bake in 350°F oven about 30 minutes, until top is lightly browned. Yield: 4-6 servings.

Sesame Seed – Native to Asia, it has a rich nut-like flavor. Used in food of ancient Persians and Egyptians; ancient Assyrians believed the gods drank Sesame Wine before creating the earth. It was regarded as a staple food by Orientals for 2000 years and as valuable as soy bean. It was brought to America by negro slaves. Used to make cooking oil and paste, also, every year tons of seed are used to make Halvah, a rich Middle Eastern candy. Toasted, sesame seed tastes like toasted almonds.

Uses: plain or toasted and in same way as nuts – pastry, cakes, cookies, cheese dishes, candy; sprinkle on appetizers, salads soups, casseroles, breads, cookies, vegetables.

Chereshnyanyk (Cherry Bars) (Ukrainian)

2 cups flour
¾ cup sugar
¼ tsp. salt
¾ tsp. baking soda
½ cup butter

1 tbsp. lemon juice
½ tsp. grated lemon rind
1 cup sour cream
1½-2 cups preserved
    cherries

Sift dry ingredients. Cut in butter. Combine lemon juice, rind and sour cream, and add to flour mixture. Mix lightly. Dough should be soft. Spoon or roll batter into 9 x 14" cake pan, and pat up side to hold filling. Save some for top. Fill pan with cherries, crisscross top with leftover dough. Bake in 350°F oven until light brown.

Alternative: Use apple filling or other fruit filling.

Mediwnyk (Honey Cake) (Ukranian)

2 cups honey
¼ lb. butter
4 eggs, beaten
1 pkg. yeast, dissolved in
    a little warm water

4 cups flour
1 tsp. baking soda
1 tsp. each cloves and cinnamon
½ lb. nuts, chopped

Bring honey to boil; add butter, then cool. Mix about ¼ of beaten eggs into dissolved yeast, then add to cooled honey. Sift dry ingredients; add to honey along with remainder of beaten eggs. Stir in nuts. Bake in large well-greased pan in 350°F oven 1 hour. "Age" several days before serving.

Kamish Brait (Marbled Bread) (Jewish)

4 eggs
1 cup sugar
1 cup corn oil
½ tsp. salt
2 tbsp. cinnamon

1 cup chopped nuts
2 heaping tsp. baking powder
3-4 cups flour (start with
    3 cups, only adding more
    to thicken well)

Cream eggs and sugar. Mix in oil and salt, then add remaining ingredients and blend well. Divide in 4 and pat into rolls. Bake in 375°F oven until brown. Cut into slices, sprinkle with cinnamon and sugar, then dry in warm oven, (200-225°F) until crisp.

Oriental

The Chinese are one of the oldest ethnic groups in Western Canada, first on the west coast, then moving east after the railway opened. They had come to North America to the California Gold Rush, later moving to the Fraser River Gold Rush in 1858. While most were looking for gold, some of the Chinese were collecting jade.

In 1891, there were only 31 Chinese in Alberta. These were the forerunners of many other Chinese who, against odds, contributed to the development of Alberta. Through their presence, they helped lay the foundation for Alberta's becoming a multiracial and multicultural society.

In the mid-19th century, China was in the throes of the Taiping Uprising, which caused a civil war with estimates of 20 million people perishing. This was the start of Chinese overseas immigration.

The first Japanese to come to Canada was Manzo Nagano. He arrived in May, 1877, at New Westminster, B.C. He was followed by Gihei Kuno who, in 1877, when he saw the Fraser River teeming with salmon, urged his fellow countrymen to follow him to Canada. Even today their descendants comprise a strong segment of the fishermen in B.C. Many of the techniques and much of the gear used in the west coast fishing industry were developed by these early immigrants.

In 1908, two East Indians, named Singh, filed a claim on land near Byemoor, Alberta. After a few months one of them died, his compatriot found it difficult to observe their tradition of cremation. Being far out at the very edge of the parkland's sparse growth of poplar, his neighbours of all nationalities rallied around and with some difficulty gathered enough stunted trees to maintain a funeral pyre.

Sikhs first became interested in Canada when a detachment of Sikh soldiers returned home to India by way of Canada after attending Queen Victoria's Diamond Jubilee in 1897. A few of them stayed in Canada.

ORIENTAL

"Mow", Chinese cook, ringing dinner bell on "CC" ranch, ca. 1905

Egg Flower Soup (Chinese)

4-6	cups chicken stock	2	cups peas
½	cup thinly sliced pork	2	eggs, lightly beaten with a fork
½	cup thinly sliced fresh mushrooms		

Heat stock to low boil. Cut pork in long ½" strips, then cut in small pieces. Add pork to stock, stir and cook. Add sliced mushrooms and peas. Stir. Keep soup at low boil. Soup can be kept hot until ready to serve. Just before serving, add beaten eggs all at once to hot soup. Eggs will come up in clumps and pieces. Stir. Serve very hot.

Bamboo Shoot Soup (Chinese)

4	oz. bamboo shoots, cut in thin strips		salt and pepper
4	dried Chinese black mushrooms	½	tsp. cornstarch mixed with a little water
4	cups chicken stock		
1	tbsp. wine vinegar	1	egg, well beaten
2	tbsp. light soy sauce	12	fresh chives, 2" slices

Blanch fresh bamboo shoots in boiling salted water for 3 minutes; drain; rinse and set aside. Soak mushrooms in warm water 15 minutes. Cook in boiling salted water 10 minutes; drain, rinse and slice in 3-4 pieces. Set aside. Bring stock to boil; add bamboo shoots, mushrooms, vinegar, soy sauce and seasonings. Simmer 10 minutes. Stir in cornstarch mixture and bring to boil. Reduce heat. Place beaten egg in strainer, add to soup by shaking back and forth over top of hot soup. Add chives and serve piping hot. Yield: 4 servings.

Chinese cuisine dates back thousands of years. The wealthy perfected it – disasters, such as droughts and floods, developed it. Because fuel and some foods were scarce, the Chinese learned to make the most of their food by using steam and chopping meat, fish and vegetables – which also made it easier to eat with chopsticks.

Tori To Negi No Suimono   *(Japanese)*

(Clear Soup with Chicken and Leeks)

4 oz. chicken breast, boned	1 tsp. sugar
salt	3¼ cups light stock
4 dried Oriental mushrooms	1 leek, finely sliced

Cut chicken in bite-size cubes, salt slightly, simmer in water to cover, until pieces are tender. Wash mushrooms, soak in warm water with sugar 20 minutes. Remove, trim stems, finely slice caps. Place chicken cubes and mushrooms in pan, add light stock, bring to boil, then simmer 5 minutes, until mushrooms are tender. Remove chicken and mushrooms from broth, place in 4 warmed soup bowls, pour broth over, and sprinkle with a few slices of leek. Serve hot.
Yield: 4 servings.

Sam Wong, Chinese businessman, New Sedalia, 1932

Tea Eggs   *(Chinese)*

6 eggs, hard-boiled
2 tsp. salt

3 tbsp. soy sauce
2 tsp. black China tea

Cook eggs 10 minutes; drain. Tap gently with spoon until the shell is covered with fine cracks. Place eggs back in pot, cover with cool water. Add rest of ingredients and bring to boil, then lower heat and simmer 1 hour. Let eggs cool in the liquid. Remove egg shells carefully, just before serving – eggs will have a marbled pattern.

Sesame Pancakes   *(Chinese)*

2 cups flour
1 cup boiling water

2 tbsp. sesame oil

Place the sifted flour in a bowl; add the water a little at a time, beating well after each addition with a wooden spoon. Knead dough 5 minutes; cover and set aside 10 minutes. Roll dough into long roll, 2" diameter, then cut in ½" slices. Roll each slice into 6" diameter pancakes. Brush tops of 2 pancakes with sesame oil and put oiled sides together like a sandwich. Do the same with remaining pancakes. Heat heavy ungreased skillet; cook doubled pancake 3 minutes on each side (some bubbles and brown spots will appear when pancake is cooked). Remove and cool slightly, then pull sandwiched pancakes apart, fold each in half, oiled side in. Stack on heat-proof dish, keep hot while cooking rest of pancakes. When all are cooked, steam in a steamer 10 minutes. Serve hot with a Chinese dinner.

Note: Pancakes will keep in refrigerator 2-3 days. Steam about 7 minutes before serving.

Tea was only discovered as a beverage in China in the 6th Century A.D., but wine was first made there 2,000 years earlier. There are many varieties of tea, but two main groups: green (unfermented) – dried in the sun; red or black (fermented) – dried by sun or air then fired over charcoal.

Curried Shrimp (Chinese)

1 lb. shrimp
ginger root
1 garlic clove, finely chopped
vegetable oil
2 tbsp. curry
salt to taste

cumin
½ onion, chopped
2 celery stalks, chopped
1 green pepper, chopped
½ cup water
1 large tbsp. cornstarch

Peel shrimp and slit down the middle, but do not cut through. Marinate with 1 slice of ginger, finely chopped, and chopped garlic. Let stand about ½ hour (stir occasionally). Fry shrimp in a little oil, add curry powder, salt to taste and 1 shake of cumin. Stir and remove from pan. Fry onion and celery for a few minutes, add green pepper and cook a few minutes longer. Add shrimp, then thicken with water mixed with cornstarch. Season to taste and serve. Yield: 4 servings.

Chrysanthemum Fish Balls (Chinese)

13 oz. boneless fish
½ tsp. salt mixed in enough
   cornflour (cornstarch) to coat fish
1 white chrysanthemum
   few slices carrots, slant sliced
   few slices/pieces green vegetables
   boiling salted water
   oil
1 shallot, thinly sliced
3 pieces green onion, 1½-2" long
   thinly sliced

1 garlic clove, finely chopped
3 slices ginger, slivered
1 tbsp. dry sherry
½ cup stock
   salt to taste
½ tsp. sugar
1 tsp. soy sauce
1 tbsp. cornstarch
¼ cup water

Wash and dry fish. Cut in thick rectangular slices. Spread salt and cornflour evenly on fish. Rinse chrysanthemum, remove petals and keep; discard rest. Blanch carrots and green vegetables in boiling salted water, with a little oil added, drain and arrange on serving platter. Reheat pan, add a little oil, brown shallots lightly, add green onions, garlic and ginger. Stir-fry briefly; add sherry, stock, a little salt and cook a few minutes. Add fish and cook briefly. Mix together sugar, soy sauce, cornflour and water. Add slowly to mixture, stir slowly and cook until thickened. Remove from heat. Add chrysanthemum petals, mix well and serve on top of vegetables on platter.

Shredded Ginger Beef   (Chinese)

½ lb. lean beef, shredded
6 tbsp. water
2 tbsp. oil
1 tbsp. soy sauce
1 tbsp. cornstarch
¼ tsp. baking soda
½ red chili pepper

¼ lb. celery, thinly sliced 1½"
6 slices ginger root, shredded
1 tsp. each soy sauce,
   cooking wine
1 tsp. each hot bean paste,
   Chinese dark vinegar
¼ tsp. each salt, sugar

Marinate shredded beef in water, oil, soy sauce, cornstarch and baking soda for 3-4 hours. Remove seeds from pepper, shred and set aside with shredded celery and ginger root. Brown beef in small amount of oil, add celery, pepper and ginger. Cover and cook on low heat until celery is just tender. Add soy sauce, wine, bean paste, vinegar, salt and sugar. Cook just to blend flavours and serve hot.

Hong Kong Chicken   (Chinese)

1 garlic clove, finely chopped
3 tbsp. oil
2½ cups cooked firm rice
1½ cups diced cooked chicken
   pepper

1½-2 cups water
1½ cups shredded lettuce
   or spinach
2 tbsp. soy sauce

Sauté garlic in oil until light brown. Stir in rice, chicken, pepper and water, just until all ingredients are moist. Bring to boil. Remove from heat; cover and let stand 5 minutes. Add lettuce or spinach and soy sauce; stir gently. Serve hot. Yield: 4 servings.

Bellevue Chinese Cafe, Lyric Theatre, Post office, hardware, hotel, pre 1917

Diced Almond Chicken   (Chinese)

2 tbsp. soy sauce
1 small ginger root
2 tbsp. sherry or gin
1 tsp. sugar
2 chicken breasts, diced
1 garlic clove, finely chopped
  oil
½ cup diced onions
½ cup diced celery

½ cup cooked peas
½ cup diced cooked carrots
½ cup diced bamboo shoots
½ cup diced mushrooms
½ cup water
½ cup chopped blanched almonds
2 tbsp. cornstarch mixed in a little
  water

Mix together soy sauce, 1 slice ginger root, finely chopped, 2 tbsp. sherry or gin, 1 tsp. sugar. Set aside. Marinate chicken with 3 slices ginger root, finely chopped and chopped garlic. Let stand ½ hour or more. Heat skillet and add a little oil. Add chicken and sauté for 2 minutes Remove from skillet. Stir-fry onion, celery, peas, carrots, bamboo shoots and mushrooms for 2 minutes. Add ½ cup water. Add soy sauce mixture, marinated chicken and almonds. Cook for a few minutes; season to taste; thicken with cornstarch and water mixture. Mix well and serve. Yield: 4 servings.

Sweet and Sour Pork   (Chinese)

2 lbs. pork, cubed
1 slice ginger root
1 garlic clove, finely chopped

2 tbsp. soy sauce
2 tbsp. cornstarch
  salt to taste

Cube pork. Combine 1 slice finely chopped ginger root and chopped garlic. Add soy sauce, cornstarch and salt. Mix well, pour over pork, let stand for ½ hour or more. Fry in hot oil until crisp.

Sweet and Sour Sauce:

3 tbsp. vinegar
3 tbsp. sugar
1 tbsp. sherry
3 tbsp. tomato paste
1½ cups water

1-2 tbsp. cornstarch
1 small onion, finely chopped
1 cup bamboo shoots, thinly sliced
1 green pepper, chopped

To make sauce, mix first 5 ingredients in a pot and bring to a boil. Thicken with cornstarch mixed in a little water. Add onion, bamboo shoots and green pepper; cook for a few minutes, then add pork and cook and stir for a few minutes more. Yield: 4 servings.

Pot Sticker Pork Dumplings   (Chinese)

Dumplings:

1½ cups flour	3 tbsp. oil
½ tsp. salt	boiling water

To make dumplings, sift flour and salt into large bowl; make well in centre. Pour in oil and enough boiling water to make a pliable dough. Use about 4 tbsp. water to start. Begin stirring with a wooden spoon, gradually incorporating flour. Add more water if needed. Knead dough 5 minutes, then set aside for ½ hour. Divide dough into 12 pieces, rolling each out to about a 6" circle.

Pork Filling:

¾ cup ground pork	½ tsp. five-spice powder
4 water chestnuts, finely chopped	1 tbsp. light soy sauce
1 tsp. sugar	1 tsp. sesame oil
3 green onions, finely chopped	

To make filling, mix all ingredients well. Place a mound of filling on half of each circle. Fold over top and press edges firmly together. Roll over joined edges using a twisting motion, press down and seal. Pour about ⅛" oil in large skillet, preferably cast-iron. When oil is hot, add dumplings, flat side down, and cook until browned and crisp*. When underside is brown, add about ⅓ cup water and cover pan tightly. Cook another 5 minutes, or until top of dumpling steams and appears cooked. Serve immediately.

Suggestion: Sprinkle with Chinese black vinegar when serving.

*Be sure dumplings are brown and crisp on bottom before adding water – to prevent sticking.

Chinese Parade, Calgary, 1905

Oyako Domburi *(Chicken and Egg on Rice)*   *(Japanese)*

1¾	cups white rice, cooked	2½	cups light stock
2	cups water	½	cup soy sauce
4	oz. chicken breast or thigh,	3	tbsp. mirin (sweet cooking wine)
4	leeks, in long thin diagonal slices	1	tbsp. sugar
4	dried Oriental mushrooms	4	eggs, lightly beaten
	warm water		

While rice is cooking, prepare rest of recipe. Cut chicken into bite-size pieces. Slice leeks. Soak mushrooms in warm water about 30 minutes; remove stems; finely slice caps. Prepare each portion separately. Measure ¼ of light stock into small frying pan; add ¼ of chicken pieces and of mushrooms. Bring to boil, then simmer 5 minutes. Add ¼ of leeks and simmer 1 minute. Season with ¼ each of soy sauce, mirin and sugar. Pour ¼ of lightly beaten eggs over chicken mixture, wait until egg is half set, then stir once. Half fill an individual serving bowl with hot rice, place cooked mixture on top just before egg is fully set (hot rice will continue to cook egg). Repeat procedure for remaining 3 portions.

Tori No Teriyaki *(Sweet Glazed Chicken)* *(Japanese)*

2	chicken legs and thighs, boned	teriyaki sauce (see below)
	vegetable oil	

Pierce chicken pieces to let sauce penetrate. Brush a little oil in frying pan and heat. Fry chicken over high heat until well browned on both sides. Remove and rinse with boiling water. Return chicken to pan, and pour Teriyaki sauce over. Cook until sauce is shiny, turning chicken so it is well coated. Remove from heat when sauce is reduced and thick. Cut chicken in ½" slices and serve hot.

Teriyaki Sauce:

1	cup soy sauce	½	cup mirin (sweet cooking wine)
1	cup sake (rice wine)	¼	cup sugar

Mix together.

Tori Gohan *(Rice with Chicken)*   *(Japanese)*

1¾	cups white rice	2	cups chicken stock
4	oz. boned chicken breast or thigh,	4	tsp. Sake (rice wine)
2	tbsp. soy sauce		fresh coriander
4	dried Oriental mushrooms		

Wash rice well, place in strainer for 30 minutes. Cut chicken in short ½" strips, sprinkle with soy sauce; marinate 30 minutes. Soak mushrooms in warm water 30 minutes, remove stems, finely slice caps. Place rice in pot, pour chicken stock and sake over, add chicken and mushroom pieces, bring to boil on high heat, stirring occasionally. Reduce heat to very low, cover and simmer 10 minutes, then turn off heat, keep covered, and let steam another 15 minutes. Mix well, serve hot and garnish with coriander. Yield: 4 servings.

Gyuniku To Broccoli No Itame-Ni   (*Japanese*)
(*Braised Beef with Broccoli*)

2 tbsp. vegetable oil
2 garlic cloves, finely sliced
4 oz. small mushrooms, halved
11 oz. broccoli, in florets

7 oz. beef sirloin, thinly sliced,
   in small pieces
1 tbsp. each sake, rice vinegar,
   sesame oil, water, sugar
2 tsp. cornstarch

Heat oil over medium heat. Add garlic, fry a few minutes Add mushrooms, sauté lightly. Stir in broccoli and beef; stir-fry to brown beef. Add rest of ingredients and bring to boil. Cover and simmer over medium heat 5 minutes, until beef is cooked, stirring occasionally to cover beef. Place on hot platter, pour a little hot stock over and serve.

Sukiyaki   (*Japanese*)
(*Beef and Vegetables simmered in Soy Sauce and Sake*)

1 lb. boneless lean beef
1 cup water
8 oz. shirataki noodles (long thin noodles)
1 large piece bamboo shoot
6 scallions, or leeks, including 3" of stem
1 medium onion, 1/2" slices
6 small mushrooms, thinly sliced
2 cakes tofu, cut in 1" cubes

2 oz. chrysanthemum leaves,
   watercress or Chinese cabbage
2" strip beef fat, folded into square
   packet
¾ cup soy sauce
9 tbsp. sugar
¾ cup sake (rice wine)

Prepare ahead: Cut beef in thin slices and halve. Bring 1 cup water to boil, drop in shirataki, return to boil, drain and cut in thirds. Cut bamboo shoot in half lengthwise, slice thinly crosswise, then rinse with cold water and drain. Slice scallions in 1½" strips diagonally. On large platter arrange beef, noodles, bamboo shoot, scallions, onion, mushrooms, tofu, greens in neat separate rows.

To Cook and Serve: This can be done at the stove, but it is very exciting done over a table burner at the table. Preheat skillet for several minutes. Rub folded fat packet over bottom of hot pan. Add 6-8 meat slices, pour in ¼ cup soy sauce, sprinkle meat with 3 tbsp. sugar, stir-fry a couple of minutes Push meat to side, add about ⅓ each of all vegetables, sprinkle with ¼ cup sake and cook 4 or 5 minutes, stirring in ⅓ of meat. With chopsticks or long-handled forks, place ingredients on individual plates. Repeat cooking procedure batch by batch. Check pan temperature occasionally – if too hot and food is sticking, lower heat, or add 1 or 2 drops of cold water.

Egg Steam Cake   *(Chinese)*

8 eggs	14 oz. flour
16 oz. sugar	¼ cup cold water (approx.)

Beat eggs with sugar until creamy yellow colour. Add flour bit by bit and at same time add water. Beat or stir by hand. Pour into bowl and steam 25-30 minutes.

Water Chestnut Pudding   *(Chinese)*

1 lb. fresh water chestnuts	8 oz. water chestnut starch
4 cups water	2 cups milk
12 oz. sugar	2 tbsp. lard

Wash and skin water chestnuts. Grate and cook in water with sugar. Mix water chestnut starch with milk, strain, then add lard and stir slowly into grated water chestnuts. Pour in oiled cake pan and steam for 1 hour

Almond Cookies   *(Chinese)*

⅔ cup butter	2 eggs
½ cup sugar	3 cups sifted flour
½ tsp. salt	1 egg yolk
1 tsp. baking soda	1 tsp. water
1 tsp. almond extract	36 blanched almonds

Have all ingredients at room temperature. Place all ingredients in mixing bowl, except the egg yolk, water and blanched almonds. Mix with the hands until well blended. Roll the dough out on a floured board. Form into 4-5 rolls about 1" in diameter. Cut off 1" pieces, and roll these into balls. Press down on a greased cookie sheet. Mix egg yolk and water. Press an almond in the top of each cookie. Brush with egg mixture. Bake in 375°F oven for 10 minutes. Makes about 4 dozen cookies.

Caramel Fruit   (Chinese)

Batter:
- 1 cup flour
- pinch of salt
- 1 egg, lightly beaten
- ¼ cup water
- ¼ cup milk

Combine all batter ingredients and beat thoroughly.

Fruit:
- 1 large apple, peeled, cored, cut in 2" cubes
- 1 large banana, cut in 1" chunks

Caramel Syrup:
- 1 cup sugar
- 3 tbsp. water
- 1 tbsp. oil

oil for deep-frying   ice water

To prepare caramel syrup combine ingredients; cook over very low heat until sugar dissolves. Bring to boil, cook rapidly until a pale colour. Use the ice water later to harden syrup.

Heat oil for deep-frying in skillet or wok. Using tongs, dip fruit in batter and fry, a few pieces at a time, until crisp. Dip battered fruit into hot syrup, coating evenly, then dip immediately into ice water to harden. Place each piece on a greased plate, then transfer to serving dish. Yield: 4 servings.

Peking Apples   (Chinese)

- 4 crisp apples
- 1 egg, lightly beaten
- ½ cup flour
- ¼ cup water
- oil for deep-frying
- ⅓ cup sugar
- 3 tbsp. oil
- 2 tbsp. water
- 3 tbsp. syrup
- 2 tsp. sesame seeds
- ice water

Peel, core and cut apples in thick slices. Blend egg, flour and ¼ cup water to make a smooth batter. Heat oil. Dip apple slices in batter and deep-fry in oil 2-3 minutes. Drain. Heat sugar, 3 tbsp. oil, 2 tbsp. water over low heat for 5 minutes. Add syrup and sesame seeds and stir for 2 minutes. Add apple pieces and stir slowly, covering each piece of apple with syrup. Using tongs, quickly dip apples into a large bowl of ice water to harden. Remove quickly and serve. Apple inside will still be hot. Yield: 4 servings.

Spice and Herb History

The first known reference to spices is in ancient Assyrian scriptures. Chiseled in stone tablets 5,000 years ago is the story that the gods drank sesame seed wine while discussing the problems of creating the earth. However, men had been acquainted with spices for possibly 50,000 years. When meat was wrapped in leaves and cooked, they learned different leaves gave different tastes. Other than drying, there was no way of keeping meat. If meat started to spoil, or was strong tasting, using leaves, grasses, bark, roots, berries, etc., helped to make the meat edible.

Eventually, some seasonings were used for medicines. Doctors of ancient Rome and Greece used various seasonings as poultices, drugs and drinks, and in religious ceremonies. Many illnesses were treated with mulled wine mixed with spices and honey.

People from most parts of the world have found plants in their regions for religious, medicinal or edible use. European forests yielded dill, marjoram, parsley, thyme, etc. Most important spices have come from various areas of South East Asia, e.g., pepper, the dried berry of a vine is found in Sumatra.

Over 2,000 years ago a flourishing spice trade, by means of camel-laden caravans, grew between the Far East and Mediterranean cities. This spice trade is referred to in the Bible. "Camels that bare spices" were the Queen of Sheba's gifts to King Solomon. Joseph's brothers sold him to spice traders. Roman soldiers took mustard seed to England in 50 B.C.

With the decline of ancient civilizations, trade and communications deteriorated between Europe and the Orient, and were not re-established for several centuries. Then the Arabs, based on the Red Sea, expanded and controlled trade from the Far East. The Prophet Mohammed married a widow whose wealth came from the spice trade. The Muslims controlled the spice trade to European centres for several hundred years, making enormous profits and adding intrigue and romance to the obtaining, transporting and trading of spices.

With Marco Polo's expeditions, Europeans rediscovered the spice trade: new overland routes were located; Columbus, Magellan and other explorers discovered sea routes; sea ports in Europe thrived. New spices, such as allspice, paprika and cayenne were discovered in the Caribbean and Central America. What was the value of these spices? A poor man's yearly wage would buy a handful of cardamom. A few handfuls of peppercorns would buy or sell a slave.

During the Renaissance, pepper, ginger and cloves from the Orient were often used with native herbs, and with sweet seasonings, such as anise, nutmeg or mint. These same spices, combinations and blends are still widely used.

In the late 18th and early 19th centuries, American sailing ships entered the spice trade. Shiploads of pepper became so numerous that the price dropped to a disastrous 3 cents a pound. Piracy in the South Seas added to the dangers of these voyages.

Seasonings were also being transported overland by settlers. For example, in Texas in the early 1800s, settlers developed chili powder, a mixture of ground peppers from Mexico. Mustard seed and some herbs were grown in California after the Gold Rush. People of many lands settled in North America, bringing their special food dishes, medicinal remedies and religions. Each of these came with a variety of uses for spices and seasonings. However, often the seasonings they had become accustomed to using were not available. This resulted in trying new uses for new plants, until, in recent years, more seasonings became available. Soldiers also brought home new ideas and tastes from countries around the world.

Today, due to modern methods of growing, mixing and packaging, many spices are available at reasonable prices. There's always a new taste treat when trying new dishes, seasonings and a variety of foods from many lands.

Allspice – Native to the Western Hemisphere, it is also called Pimento, Jamaica Pepper, Jamaica Pimento. It tastes like a blend of cloves, cinnamon and nutmeg. Used by Aztecs and Mayans, allspice was discovered in the New World by Columbus and taken to Europe in the 1500s by Spaniards.

> Uses: whole – soups, stews, sauces, pickles, stewed fruit, pot roasts, fish; ground – cakes, cookies, fruit puddings and pies, mincemeat, spaghetti sauce, soups, pickled eggs, sweet potatoes.

Anise seed – Native to the Mediterranean area, it is also grown in Mexico, Spain, Syria, China, S. Russia, Turkey. It tastes like strong licorice. Anise was taxed by King Edward I for revenue to repair London Bridge. It flavors the Greek liqueur, Ouzo, and the Spanish liqueur, Anisette.

> Uses: whole or crushed – cakes, cookies, breads, sausage, beverages, baked apples, stewed fruits, pickled fish, deviled eggs, poultry.

Basil – Native to India and also northern Mediterranean countries, it has a very fragrant, clove-like aroma. Said to have been cut only by Kings with a Golden Sickle, thus it was called the "Herb of Kings" by ancient Greeks. Worshiped in India, it was brought to Europe in the 10th century. 'It's said in certain European countries that when a girl pins a sprig of basil on a boy it is "all over but the wedding bells".

> Uses: tomato and egg dishes, pasta, stuffings, stews, meat, fish, soups, vegetables.

Bay Leaves – Native to the Mediterranean area, they are also called Laurel Leaves. Strong and pungent, they are usually removed from cooked food before serving. Ancient Greeks gave laurel, or bay, wreaths to winners of Olympic Games, victors in battle, honored poets were known as "poets laureate", a term still used today.

> Uses: soups, pickles, fish, omelettes, custards, used in water to cook vegetables, roasts, stews, tomato sauces.

Caraway Seed – Native to Europe, Iran, Turkey; from Ancient Arabic word "karawya", it is a type of parsley with a lightly sweet, licorice taste. One of the oldest spices, it is recorded in medical papyrus from Thebes about 1550 B.C.; was used in cooking by ancient Greeks and Romans. Kummel, a caraway-flavored liqueur is popular in Germany.

> Uses: appetizers, fish, chicken, goose, roasts, breads, sweet desserts, cabbage, sauerkraut, potatoes, stewed apples, soups, stews, marinades; sprinkle on salads.

Cardamom – Native to India, it also comes from Guatemala. It has pungent, aromatic, sweet flavor. Grown by a King of Babylon about 700 B.C. it was used by early Egyptians, ancient Greeks and Romans in perfumes, and is used in the cosmetic industry today. First brought to Europe by old caravans, it is the third most expensive spice after saffron and vanilla. It is the main spice in Danish pastry.

> Uses: cakes, gingerbread, fruit dishes, curry powder, pickling spice, beverages, puddings, sweet potatoes, hot spiced wines, sweet sauces, pickled herring.

Chili Powder – A variety of blends of spices, it is native to Mexico and has a pungent, slightly sweet taste. Aztecs used a similar blend about 9,000 years ago. Columbus took some to Europe, the Portuguese took it to India and Africa. In the 1600's it was brought back to America by Europeans. It is a "must" in Mexican food.

> Uses: chili, sauces, egg dishes, stews, meatloaf, corn dishes, marinades, dips.

Cinnamon – Native to Sri Lanka, the term refers to several species grown in S.E. Asia. It is called cassia in Burma. Sweet, pungent and spicy, it was used in Ancient China and called "kwei". Cinnamon was used in perfumes by Egyptian Queen Hatshepsut, about 1500 B.C.; God told Moses to use it in making holy oil.

> Uses: whole – pickling, vegetable and fruit dishes, drinks, stir sticks; ground – breads, puddings, cakes, vegetable and meat dishes, preserves, eggnog, puddings.

Cloves – Native to Zanzibar, Madagascar and Indonesia, clove comes from the Latin 'clavus', meaning 'nail'. It has a sweet, pungent, almost hot taste. During the Chinese Han Dynasty (206 B.C. to 200 A.D.), courtiers addressing the Emperor had to hold cloves in their mouth. Seeds of the clove tree were stolen from the Dutch in the 18th Century to try to break the Dutch monopoly on the spice trade.

> Uses: whole – ham, fruit, glazed pork, corned beef, pickled eggs, beverages, fish, sauces, pickling, soups, pomander balls; ground – cakes, puddings, stewed fruit, some vegetables, sauces, mincemeat, soups, beverages.

Coriander/Cilantro – Native to S. Europe and Mediterranean areas, it is also grown in Argentina. Coriander is seeds and powder; Cilantro is fresh leaves. It tastes slightly lemony. Recorded in medical papyrus from Thebes about 1550 B.C., it was used in love potions by ancient Greeks and Romans.

> Uses: whole – punch, sweet pickles, hot drinks; ground – candies, cookies, breads, cakes, Danish pastry, fish, chicken, pork, meatloaf, egg sauces, vegetable soups, stewed fruit, stews, fruit and meat sauces.

Cumin – Native to the Mediterranean area, it has a strong, earthy taste and was used in drugs by Babylonian and Assyrian doctors. Used by ancient Greeks and Romans to preserve foods, and by Romans as a substitute for Black Peppercorns, they also ground it into a paste to spread on breads. The main ingredient in chili and curry powders, it can be substituted for caraway seed.

> Uses: whole or ground – cheese dishes, chili, eggs, meatloaf, stews, soups, sauces, sauerkraut, cookies, breads, potatoes, beans, rice, wild game and fowl.

Curry Powder – One of the oldest spice blends, this originated in India. The taste and 'hotness' varies depending on mixes of spices.

> Uses: meats, fish, poultry dishes, hamburger dishes, eggs, sauces, soups, casseroles, some vegetables, dips, rice.

Dill – Native to Europe, it has an aromatic, pungent and distinct flavor. Babylonian and Assyrian doctors used it in drugs. Ancient Greeks used it as a remedy for hiccups; for Romans it was a symbol of vitality. In Middle Ages it was believed to protect against witchcraft and used in magic potions. Available as seed and leaves (weed).

> Uses: seed – pickles, salads, sauerkraut, egg dishes, soups, sauces, stews, breads, lamb, fish, chicken, sausage; weed – sauces, pickles, egg dishes, vegetables, fish, rice, cheese dishes, pasta.

Fennel – Native to the Mediterranean area, it is aromatic with a slight licorice flavor. Used in drugs by ancient Babylonian and Assyrian doctors, it was also used by ancient Romans and Greeks and known in ancient China and India. Called "meetin' seed" by Puritans, they chewed the seeds in church. It is a favorite seasoning in Italian baking.

> Uses: fish, pork, stews, vegetables, cheese and egg dishes, pickles, stewed apples, soups, tomato sauces, cakes, cookies.

Garlic – Native to S. Europe, S. Siberia and Central Asia, it has a distinctive taste and aroma. Prized as a food by ancient Greeks and Romans, it was eaten by Egyptian slaves who built the Pyramids. Ancients believed the smell drove away serpents and scorpions; Hippocrates warned it was bad for the eyes but good for the body. It is available in powder, salt, chips, minced, juice.

> Uses: vegetable, meat, fish dishes, soups, dips, sauces, pickles, butters, marinades.

Ginger – Native to S.E. Asia, it has been cultivated for over 3000 years. It is grown in Africa and the W. Indies. It has a hot, spicy, sweet taste. Marco Polo found it in China. One of first Oriental spices known in Europe, it was used in the Middle East and Europe before the early Romans. The Spanish took it to the West Indies and trade resulted with Jamaica in the 1500s. It is available fresh, dried, in syrup and crystals.

    Uses: whole – pickles, beverages, marinades, stewed fruit, sauces, tea, ginger beer; ground – cakes, cookies, bread, puddings, Oriental dishes, meat, poultry, most vegetables, chutney, sauces, soups, sweet potatoes, pickles, stewed fruit, punch. Crystallized (fresh root cooked in syrup) used as a confection or condiment.

Hyssop – Native to the Mediterranean area, it has a slightly bitter taste with a hint of mint. Boiled with honey, ancient Greeks used it as a cough remedy. It is mentioned in the Bible from Moses to John the Baptist. It flavors the French Liqueur Chartreuse, available as fresh or dried leaves or flowers. (Do not use together – the flavor of the leaves overtakes that of the flowers).

    Uses: dried or fresh leaves – soups, stews, teas, sauces, pastas; sprinkle fresh leaves or flowers on salads.

Mace – Imported from Indonesia and the West Indies, it was mentioned in Denmark and Europe at end of the 12th Century and may have been used earlier. Mace is the bright red lacy skin covering the shell of nutmeg. It has a similar flavour to nutmeg but more delicate. Mace and nutmeg are the only two spices found naturally on the same plant.

    Uses: whole or ground – cakes, breads, hot and cold drinks, puddings, pies, soups, meat, fish, fish stews, poultry, sauces, apple dishes, vegetables, cheese spreads and dishes, Danish pastries.

Marjoram – Native to the Mediterranean area, it is also grown in Central America. It has a distinct aroma and a slightly bitter but pleasant taste. Used by the ancient Egyptians it was also used in medicine by Hippocrates and during the Middle Ages. A symbol of happiness to ancient Greeks, it was used to crown newlyweds.

    Uses: meats, poultry, fish, tomato dishes, vegetables, sauces, egg dishes, soups.

Mint – Native to Europe and Asia, it has an aromatic, sweet taste with a cool aftertaste. It was used by ancient Assyrians in Fire-God rituals. Named by the Greeks after the mythical character Minthe; it has long been associated with romance.

    Uses: punches, teas, dessert sauces, lamb stew, jelly, meat and fish sauces, fruit soup, cake, chocolate drinks and desserts, puddings, potatoes, peas, carrots, garnish.

Mustard – Native to Europe and S.W. Asia, it has a pungent flavour. It has been used in medicine and as a condiment since the days of the ancient Greeks and Romans.

    Uses: seed – sauerkraut, cabbage, creamed soups, potato salad, pickles, vegetable relishes, corned beef; dry (powdered) – egg and cheese dishes, vegetables, appetizers, sauces, meats, poultry.

Nutmeg – Native to Indonesia, it has a sweet and spicy taste. The outer shell is mace. It reached Europe by the 12th century; the Portuguese, then Dutch, controlled the spice trade (nutmeg, cinnamon, pepper, etc.) for centuries.

    Uses: ground or grated – cakes, cookies, pastries, sprinkled over hot or cold drinks, eggnog, puddings, soups, fruit, vegetables, sauces, meats, poultry, fish.

Oregano – Native to the Mediterranean area, it is also grown in Mexico and used in chili. The name is Greek, means "joy of the mountains", where wild varieties grow. Oregano is a wild variety of marjoram, it has a strong and aromatic flavour, a slightly bitter but pleasant taste. Many wild varieties grow in Greece, called 'rigani', they are stronger flavored and coarser than ordinary oregano or marjoram. Used by the ancient Romans, it was practically unknown in America until after W.W.II. It is a main spice in pizza.

Uses: tomato dishes, chili, stews, vegetable soups, egg and cheese dishes, stuffing, meat and pasta sauces, poultry, fish.

Paprika – Central American, paprika is red, mild, slightly sweet; Hungarian paprika is lighter in colour and more pungent. Plants were taken to Europe by early Spanish explorers. A Nobel Prize was won by a Hungarian scientist for research in the vitamin content of Paprika. It is the main seasoning in Hungarian goulash.

Uses: stews, casseroles, chicken, veal, sprinkle on fish, meats, soups, eggs, cheese dishes, cream sauces, appetizers.

Parsley – Native to Mediterranean shores, it has a mild aroma and pleasant taste. Used by Europeans in and on foods since about 300 B.C., it was brought to America by colonists. It is said the seed must go seven times to the Devil and back before sprouting.

Uses: in and on appetizers, soups, salads, spreads, sauces, meats, poultry, fish, potatoes, egg dishes.

Pepper – Native to the East Indies, it is also grown in Mexico, Brazil, Japan, Nigeria. It has a hot, pungent and biting taste. The World's most popular spice, it accounts for ¼ of the world spice trade. White and black pepper was used by ancient Greeks and Romans. In 5th century Rome, a ransom demand was 3000 lbs. of pepper; Arabs grew rich supplying pepper to Rome. The Pepperers Guild was founded in London about 1180 A.D. Marco Polo wrote of the use of large quantities of pepper in China. It is available in whole black, white, red, green, fine ground white and black, coarse ground black, cracked black. It is not used in sweets, except for the German Christmas cookie "Pfeffernusse".

Uses: whole or cracked in peppermills – ground over foods being prepared or after serving; whole – pickling, sauces, soups, stews, some dressings, marinades, meats; white – in light-coloured sauces, soups, Oriental dishes (can be substituted for black).

Red Pepper – Native to tropical America and the West Indies, it has a hot pungent flavor. Known in pre-Inca days, it was found in Cuba by Columbus, who took it to Europe. Available crushed and ground, it is popular in Mexican and Italian food.
Cayenne – a powdered form.

Uses: powdered – meats, poultry, fish, deviled eggs, omelets, soups, cheese dishes, chili, stews, pickles, sauces, curried dishes, dips; crushed – pickling, gumbos, sauces, sausage.

Poppy Seed – Native to S.W. Asia, it has a nut-like flavor. Seeds used are ripe seeds. It comes from the opium poppy but has no narcotic properties. Medicinal derivatives (opium, morphine, codeine) come from the sap of unripe seed pods. In 1500 B.C., it was grown by Egyptians as a source of cooking oil and opium was used for medicinal purposes. It was not used as an abused narcotic until the 1800s when smoking opium became popular, mainly in China. The best quality poppy seeds are grown by the Dutch. Used widely in Slavic and Hungarian baking.

Uses: cottage cheese, eggs, pastry, cakes, cookies, breads, fruit salad dressings; sprinkle on breads, cookies, cakes, casseroles, fruit salads, some vegetables.

Rosemary – It is native to the Mediterranean area. Latin means 'dew of the sea', as it thrives near salt sea spray in a warm, dry climate. It has a sweet woody flavour. Used about 500 B.C.; in folklore it will only grow in gardens of the righteous; "There's rosemary, that's for remembrance" by Ophelia in "Hamlet"; even today, it is placed on graves of heroes in England. Used by colonists to scent soaps, it is also called "Rosa Maria".

Uses: lamb dishes, fish, fish sauces, poultry, wild fowl and game, soups, stews, vegetables, fruits, breads, egg dishes.

Saffron – Native to the Mediterranean area, it comes from the saffron crocus plant. It has a pleasant bitter taste. It was used by ancient Assyrians for medicinal purposes; in medical papyrus of Thebes, about 1550 B.C. It is believed the Phoenician traders brought it to Spain and England. The most expensive spice in the world, it requires 75,000 blossoms, or 225,000 stigmas to make 1 lb. It is widely used in French, Spanish and South American cooking.

Uses: usually crushed – breads, cakes, rice, soups, sauces, seafood and chicken dishes.

Sage – Native to the Mediterranean area, the best quality is from Yugoslavia. Very aromatic, slightly bitter, it was used by ancient Assyrians, Greeks and Romans as a tonic and for snakebite. In the Middle Ages it was used in medicines and as a "cure-all" tonic. Available ground, rubbed and dried leaves.

Uses: stuffings, biscuits, meats, poultry, fish, sausage, chowders, beans, tomatoes, onions, potatoes, sauces.

Salt – Known since prehistoric times, it was used in religious rites by ancient Greeks, Romans, Hebrews, Christians, also as a medium of exchange. In the Old Testament, it was used as an offering to God. It was subject to severe taxation in ancient China. Because of its usefulness as a preservative it was used by ancients as a symbol of enduring faith. In ancient Ethiopia and Tibet salt was made into cubes and used as money. In Ancient Rome, salt was valued highly; soldiers were given a salt allowance, in Latin "salarium", thus the term "'salary". Available in rock crystals, refined, sea salt.

Uses: essential in diets of humans and warm-blooded animals, it is in most foods, naturally or added, preservative, dyeing, making soap and glass.

Savory – Native to the Mediterranean area, it is aromatic and pungent. Known to Hippocrates for its medicinal uses; ancient Romans made a mint – like sauce of savory and vinegar. In the Middle Ages it was used in puddings, pies, cakes.

Uses: stuffings, egg dishes, poultry, meatloaf, stews, sauces, soups, some vegetables, sauerkraut, rice; sprinkle on cooked fish.

Tarragon – Native to West and South Asia, Siberia, it has been grown since the Middle Ages in France. In Latin it means "Little Dragon", from the Medieval belief it would cure venomous bites. Very aromatic, it has a hint of anise flavour. It was a cherished herb of ancient Greeks and Egyptians. It flavors Tarragon vinegar and is the distinctive flavor in Bearnaise sauce.

Uses: mayonnaise, cream sauces, tuna salads and casseroles, meat sauces, poultry, fish, meats, egg dishes; sprinkle on salads.

Thyme – Native to the Mediterranean area, it has an aromatic and slightly pungent flavor. Used in medicines by ancient Assyrian doctors and chemists; ancient Greeks and Romans used it to flavour cheese and liquor. In ancient times it was believed thyme would only grow near the sea. It was brought to America in the early 1700s. It flavors Benedictine liqueur.

Uses: meats, poultry, fish, with butter over vegetables and fish, stuffing, sauces, cheese, egg and tomato dishes, clam chowder; sprinkle on fresh vegetables.

Turmeric – Native to China, it is also grown in India and the West Indies. It has a musky odor and is slightly bitter. Cultivated over 2,000 years in India, China and Middle East, it was believed used in sun worship by ancient Persians. It was written about by an early Greek physician, in 1st Century, A.D. Used as a dye, today it is used to colour butter, cheese, pickles, East Indian foods, curries and mustards. It is a major ingredient in curry powder and prepared mustard.

Uses: pickles, mayonnaise, cream sauces, egg and rice dishes, soups, chicken, fish.

Photographs Courtesy of Glenbow Archives

Front Cover	Mary Fraser, Fort Chipewyan, ca. 1903	– NA-2617-60
First People	Naomi Little Walker, Blackfoot, late 1890s	– NA-1773-28
	Mrs. Black Eagle, Mrs. Buck Running Rabbit,	
	Mrs. Wolf Leg, n.d.	– NA-768-4
	Blood warriors and wives, 1892	– NA-668-20
	Woman with horse & travois near Gleichen, ca. 1880s	– NA-403-2
North American	Alice Gardner, at Wineglass ranch, North of Brockett,	
	early 1900s	– NA-4035-197
	Democrat load of Saskatoon pickers near Stavely, 1909	– NA 666-10
	Binder operating on Basilici ranch, Kew, 1913	– NA-3917-23
	Picnic, Dog Pound Creek area, early 1900s	– NA-2194-3
British Isles	Shirley Rourke cooking supper in Bragg Creek	– NA-5157-2
	Albert Armstrong family, Conjuring Creek, 1906	– NA-4174-31
	Hauling Water, Lucky Strike district, early 30s	– NA-2616-8
	Mrs. Ings, at Midway ranch, Nanton, ca. 1911	– NA-2368-6
Scandinavian	Mrs. E.P. Oveson, Floram area, ca. 1914	– NA-2616-15
	Erikson family and friends, Veteran area, 1910	– NA-4190-2
	Mrs. and Mrs. Lokken, Viking area, 1918	– NA-3543-32
	Van Meter and Erickson Families, ca. 1906	– NA-4174-29
Western European	Mrs. L.C. Eckenfelder and children, Trochu, 1915	– NA-3018-49
	Mme. Corine Joly, St. Paul, 1929	– NA-4394-6
	Group at Paul de Beaudrap's ranch, Trochu, 1905	– NA-3018-36
	Picnic lunch while ploughing, Neutral Hills, 1910	– NA-3747-6
Central European	Jane Rummel, Basilici ranch, Kew, 1911	– NA-3917-19
	Meat Market and Post Office, Seven Persons, 1911	– NA-3729-26
	Carrying Christmas tree home, Kew, 1926	– NA-3917-29
	Thresher's dinner, Rosyth district, 1913	– NA-2284-15
Eastern European	Mrs. Theresa Ully, outside homestead, Ully, ca. 1915	– NA-2616-22
	Mr. & Mrs. D. Bilej, from Romania, Shandro, 1903	– NA-2828-6
	Hutterites, Rockyford area, 1919	– NA-4079-75
	Russian Settlers, Unity, Saskatchewan, n.d.	– NA-3035-32
Oriental	"Mow", Chinese cook, ringing dinner bell at "CC"	
	ranch, ca. 1905	– NA-4571-29
	Sam Wong, Chinese businessman, New Sedalia, 1932	– NA-1978-1
	Bellevue Chinese Cafe, Lyric, Theatre, Post office,	
	hardware, hotel, pre-1917	– NA-3903-1
	Chinese Parade, Calgary, 1905	– NA-1497-9

Recipes donated and tested by members and friends of The Southern Alberta Pioneers and Their Descendants

Mae Alexander
Brigette Amsterdam
Kay Babiuk
Vi Baskill
Dorothy Cavanagh
Barbara Cherniwchen
Al Collins
Evelyn (Hardwick) Calow
Congressional House of Jacob –
  Mikveh Israel
Dorrie Coyle
Jean Cuthbert
Maria Violet Czeman
Eleanor Danielson
Joan Davis
Fern Dorsch
Jean Dudley
Sally Erdman
Mrs. Estrella
Muriel Facey
Rose Farargo
Ruth Galloway
Betty & Gil Goddard
Dorothe Goddard
Herbert W. Gold
Juliette Iperhoff
Andrew Jirach (from his
  grandmother in Prague)

Sandra Laine
Donna Leslie
Hazel Lienhart
Helen Mackie
Margaret MacLean
Edweena Mair
Gwen McGinnis
Deloras Myck
Shirley Nichol
Muriel Nicholson
Nancy Palmer (from her Grandma
  Hester de Boshen, in Holland)
Maureen Peckham
Carole Peteherych
Betty Ann Schmaltz
Alice Schwieger
Dixie Shah
Donna Shaw
Madeleine Tam
Lucille Togstad
Doreen Turning-Robe (Daughter
  of Chief David Crowchild)
Elizabeth and Richard Urch
Olive Urch
Anne Vincent
Warren Vincent
Pat Waite
Jan Worger

Southern Alberta Pioneers and Their Descendants

Cookbook Committee

Vi Baskill
Fern Dorsch
Sally Erdman
Muriel Facey
Ruth Galloway
Helen Mackie
Edweena Mair

Maureen Peckham
Carole Peteherych
Alice Schwieger
Betty Ann Schmaltz
Dixie Shah
Anne Vincent

Index

Share *PIONEER KITCHENS* with a Friend

Order *PIONEER KITCHENS* at $16.95 per book plus $4.00 (total order)
for postage and handling:

PIONEER KITCHENS _____ x $16.95 = $_____

Handling Charge _____ $___4.00___

Subtotal: _____ $_____

In Canada add 7% G.S.T. _____ (subtotal x .07) = $_____

Total enclosed_____ $_____

Name_____

Street: _____

City: _____ Province/State:_____

Country:_____ Postal Code/Zip Code:_____

Please make cheque payable or money order to: Southern Alberta Pioneers
3625 – 4th St. S.W.
Calgary, Alberta   Canada   T2S 1Y3

International orders payable in U.S. funds./Price is subject to change.
For fund raising or volume rates, contact SOUTHERN ALBERTA PIONEERS.
Please allow 3-4 weeks for delivery

Share *PIONEER KITCHENS* with a Friend

Order *PIONEER KITCHENS* at $16.95 per book plus $4.00 (total order)
for postage and handling:

PIONEER KITCHENS _____ x $16.95 = $_____

Handling Charge _____ $___4.00___

Subtotal: _____ $_____

In Canada add 7% G.S.T. _____ (subtotal x .07) = $_____

Total enclosed_____ $_____

Name_____

Street: _____

City: _____ Province/State:_____

Country:_____ Postal Code/Zip Code:_____

Please make cheque payable or money order to: Southern Alberta Pioneers
3625 – 4th St. S.W.
Calgary, Alberta   Canada   T2S 1Y3

International orders payable in U.S. funds./Price is subject to change.
For fund raising or volume rates, contact SOUTHERN ALBERTA PIONEERS.
Please allow 3-4 weeks for delivery